KELLE LIMA

LILITH FLETCHER

AND THE
THREADS OF FATE

 WRITERVERSE JOURNEY L.L.C.

Author: Lima, Kelle
Illustrators: Chaves, Allan | Lima, Kelle
Title: Lilith Fletcher and the Threads of Fate
Series: Book 1 of the Lilith Fletcher Series
Description: Taylorsville: Writerverse Journey LLC, 2025. | Audience: Ages 10-14
Library of Congress Control Number: 2025902850

ISBNs: 978-1-960656-08-7 (paperback) | 978-1-960656-09-4 (hardcover) | 978-1-960656-07-0 (eBook)
Subjects: Greek Mythology, Friendship, Hidden Worlds, Female Protagonist, Fantasy - Juvenile literature

To all the girls who feel like outsiders—may you one day step into a world where you truly belong.

KEEPERS OF THE FLAME

First of all, my deepest apologies—this story has been in the making for over a decade, and the number of incredible people to thank is as vast as the stars in the night sky.

To my daughter, Julia, the wise and wonderful guiding force in my life. Every day with you is a divine adventure.

To my mom, Mirian, my number one fan—truly, you reached more people during my last launch than Hermes himself delivering messages! Your unwavering belief in me means the world.

To my sisters, Soraya, Sabrine, and Géssica, who each bring their own kind of magic. Soraya, for lifting me up like Atlas holding the sky when I was at my lowest. Sabrine, for always being the healer, like Apollo. And Géssica, for inspiring me with kindness, as warm and constant as Hestia's hearth.

To my family and friends in Brazil, whose love has been a guiding light. Ana Paula, for listening even before I had anything to say. Allan Brito, for granting me access to as much knowledge as Metis has. Luciana, Sérgio Paulo, tia Ruth, tia Hortência, Alice, Ludmilla, Sílvia, tio Fá, Xande, and Danilo—you all mean more to me than the Golden Fleece itself. Ângela and FJ, for meeting "Arthur" before anyone else and being my first real writing partners.

To my Salt Lake City family—Emily, Ed, Alex, and Adam—thank you for making this place feel like Mount Olympus and for filling my days with light.

Aparant, John, Gabe, and Anton—your support across the distance these past few years has meant everything. Like Daedalus, you've helped me navigate the labyrinth.

Sílvio Campello, for igniting my passion for publishing during my undergrad, and Corrinne Lewis, for keeping that spark alive.

Allan Chaves, without your stunning illustrations, this book wouldn't shine as brightly. You are a true artist, overflowing with talent.

To the writing community, especially Jennifer, Carli, and Melanie—you are more than fellow writers; you are cherished friends. And to April for believing in me, giving so much back to the community, and helping me grow as a writer each day.

To my incredible alpha and beta groups, who sliced my book into pieces with sharp swords of feedback—ha! A special thanks to Kylee and Jacob for the final surveys that helped shape the final touches of this story. You are the strategists and warriors who stood by me on this quest.

And finally, to you, dear reader—thank you for being here. May Lilith Fletcher's adventure fill your heart with as much wonder as it did mine.

CONTENTS

CHAPTER ONE

AN UNEXPECTED BIRTHDAY

L ilith's cake was perfect—fourteen cherries on top, and a swirling silver candle on the side. Her mouth watered at the thought of taking a bite right there in the middle of the bakery. However, she had to be back home before Meghan finished bathing Amy. Her stepmom was lovely, but she always treated Lilith like Sleeping Beauty on the verge of pricking her finger.

Nothing, absolutely nothing, would stop Lilith from having a cake this year. Four years in a row without one was enough. If her dad was too busy and wouldn't make it to the bakery before closing time, she'd handle it herself, permission or not.

"Thank you," Lilith said to the stubby lady behind the counter, her voice trembling with excitement as the shop's door jingled on her way out. The sun had just set, but the evening was darker than usual.

"Brr," Lilith muttered as the wind flung her hood back and raindrops began soaking her hair. *Where was that knitting lady who'd been sitting on the porch of that peach-colored house earlier?* Nowhere to be seen. In fact, Lilith hadn't spotted anyone for the past two blocks. *That was a little unusual, wasn't it?* Even for a rainy day.

The streetlight flickered. Then, *splash!* Cold water seeped into Lilith's tennis shoes, soaking her toes.

"Ewww!" Lilith wrinkled her nose, shaking her skinny leg. *Only two more blocks. I've got this!* She straightened her back, the only part of her that was still dry thanks to her backpack.

The wet sidewalk reflected a zigzagging light. She narrowed her eyes, trying to track it. Suddenly, a loud screech tore through the air. A car careened toward her like it was on a skating rink.

People say that in life-threatening moments, you run or scream, but Lilith froze. She couldn't even blink. Her heart clenched.

A flash of bright blue particles burst out of nowhere, and a boy popped up in front of her. The car slammed him right above the waist and he tumbled over the hood, landing beside Lilith. Then the driver jerked the wheel and disappeared around the next corner, tires screeching again.

Splat. Her arms went numb, letting her precious birthday cake fall. *Had she died? No.* Breath shaky, her eyes settled on the boy sprawled next to the curb as his hoodie soaked up a spreading crimson patch. He looked a couple of years older than she was.

Why had she gone to the bakery? If she hadn't, none of this would've happened. A strangled grunt snapped Lilith out of her own terror.

The boy's thick brows pulled together, pain carving lines into his face with every breath. Lilith took a shaky step closer. *Did she know him?* Something was familiar, but she couldn't quite place it.

A sharp, high-pitched ringing tore through her head. Lilith clapped her hands over her ears but the sound cut off as suddenly as it started, leaving her dazed.

The boy. Focus. She told herself, forcing air into her lungs, the way you do when you can't afford to fall apart. "It's g-gonna be fine," she said it aloud this time, aiming for steady and landing on thin. She dropped to her knees beside him and yanked her backpack open. "Phone. Phone... Where are you?"

"I'm—I'm... sorry," the boy croaked. "A-accept your gift."

Lilith blinked. *Accept my gift? Is he hallucinating?*

"Sure, I do. I accept my gift," she replied, trying to keep him conscious. She held his hand and dug deeper for her phone with the other. "Stay with me, I'll call for help. It'll be okay," she insisted.

"It'll be okay," the boy fumbled something onto her wrist. A necklace. Its pendant was shaped like an infinity symbol and glowed faintly.

What on earth? Lilith tilted her head.

"Sorry, L," he rasped. Lilith's heart clenched. Did he say "L," as in her initial? She inhaled sharply as he released the pendant, and a neon flash seared across her wrist. *Was she losing her mind? What had just happened? And, more importantly, why did he become so quiet?*

"No. No, no, no!" Lilith roared, reaching for his shoulder, tears burning her eyes. But the necklace yanked her left arm back, as if it was stuck...on something invisible. Wiping her face, she tried to figure out how her arm could possibly be trapped. Lilith traced it with her right hand, searching for hidden strings but found nothing except for the pendant resting on top of her wrist.

"Help!" she shouted, with the necklace seared against her skin, burning white-hot.

Whoosh. The boy's body shot upright in a single horrifying jerk. Gold sand swirled out of him, funneled into the pendant over Lilith's wrist, and then it glowed blue. Her screams ricocheted down the empty street. *This was a nightmare. It had to be.* But if the throbbing pain in her wrist couldn't wake her, no pinch in the world would do the job.

The sand spun faster and faster inside the glass, a solid glow forming. Then the boy's limp form collapsed onto the ground.

It took Lilith a few seconds to process what she'd just witnessed. She tried reaching for her backpack, but it lay too far. So, she glanced at the boy. "Sorry." Lilith winced and leaned in to pat his pockets. "A phone!" she gasped. Only to stifle a second gasp when his lock screen lit up: a photo of seven-year-old Lilith. *Why would he have a picture of her as a child?*

"Ow!" Her wrist sizzled, and she slammed the phone against the pendant in reflex. "No!" she cried, terrified she'd crushed the only chance to call for help as the device's screen cracked and became unresponsive.

While the shimmering grains hummed inside the glass pendant over Lilith's wrist, defeat overtook her. The world became a blur until the sand stopped moving. Each swirl draining her energy until, at last, the pendant let go of her arm and both fell onto the asphalt. She blinked once and focused on the infinity symbol still glowing on her skin. She blinked again and found the boy's pale face beside her, eyes empty. *Do I know you?* A half-formed memory nagged at the edges of her mind.

But the shrill noise from a moment ago returned. Her vision swam. Right before passing out, she glimpsed a shape in the darkness. *Help!* she wished she could scream, but she was too weak to force the words out. Then everything turned black.

Chapter Two

THE WORST GIFT

Beeping echoed in Lilith's ears as she tried to take in her surroundings, but the harsh light stung her eyes, forcing them shut. There was a smell of latex, coffee, and disinfectant—definitely a hospital. She knew the routine. Her dad was a doctor, so she'd spent more time in waiting rooms than in bedrooms most of her life. At least until he married Meghan.

Lilith's head spun with murky fragments of memory: the car, the boy. Slowly, she peeled her eyes open. Hospital curtains, beep of machines... For a second, relief flooded her. *Maybe the boy from the accident was there too, alive. Was that a possibility?*

Meghan stood by the window, her curly copper hair spilling from a messy bun. Her stepmom adjusted her hearing aid, then resumed fiddling with something out of sight. When she finally turned around, relief softened her face.

Lilith tried to wave, but her limbs felt like jelly—too heavy to lift.

"She's awake!" Meghan signed with one sharp, oversized motion while yanking Nicholas closer by the sleeve of his white coat.

Her dad's glasses slid down his nose as he approached with a stern frown. "What were you thinking?" Nicholas barked, his hands signing almost as frantically as he spoke. "Wandering around without telling anyone you were leaving? No note? Almost getting yourself killed?" His fingers ran through his black hair, but the stubborn locks fell back over his squared glasses. "And on your birthday of all days?" he complained.

Lilith wasn't sure whether he was angry or worried—perhaps somewhere in between. Her birthday had always been a bittersweet reminder of her mom's death anniversary, since Katherine had died giving birth to her. And as Lilith grew older and began to resemble her mother more, it became even harder for Nicholas to bear.

"I just...I just wanted a cake this year," Lilith gave in, tears welling up. "I'm really sorry," her voice was barely audible. "Dad," she took a shaky breath before lifting her eyes. "What about the boy? Is he okay?"

"Boy?" Nicholas crossed his arms.

"The one who got hit by the car," Lilith explained. "When he saved me I tried—"

"Honey, you were the one hit," Meghan signed gently, eyebrows knitting together.

"What? No. He saved me. I—I mean," Lilith stammered, confusion swirling in her voice. "He popped out of nowhere and said something about a gift. Then it burned me! Look," she fought back, lifting her arm, but the glowing infinity symbol wasn't there.

Nicholas shook his head. "I'm sure you're feeling confused," he said, glancing at his watch. "You probably dreamed it. Pain can make our minds do strange things." He offered a small shrug. "This conversation isn't over, but right now, you need rest. And I have a few patients to check on. So lie back, and we'll talk later, okay?" he said, and without waiting for an answer, he waved before stepping out.

"Are you okay?" Meghan signed, sinking into the chair by Lilith's bed.

"Yeah," Lilith replied, moving her fist up and down. "Meghan?" she called with a wave.

"What?" Her stepmom cocked her head.

"I'm sorry," Lilith signed with a sigh, sinking into her pillow. "I didn't mean to—"

"Don't worry. I'm just happy you're okay." Meghan winked, rolled her neck, and closed her eyes.

Lilith wanted to say more, but she didn't know how. She tried relaxing but images from the night before rushed in—flashes of the accident, the glowing pendant, the sand, the empty eyes.

She clutched her wrist, hoping for some kind of proof, something real she could point to. But there was nothing.

Meghan dozed off in minutes. Lilith fought the urge to wake her, guilt gnawing at her for sneaking out in the first place. *How could her stepmom be so calm about everything?* Lilith had been bracing for a massive lecture. Instead, Meghan gave her calm.

Lilith stared at the ceiling, her mind drifting. *What did they mean by "no boy"?* A frown grew on her face.

She could still picture every detail of him. And couldn't stop replaying everything that happened in her head—the car, the infinity-shaped pendant, the rain, the shimmering sand, the pain. *How was there no trace of any of that? How could her mind make all of this up?* But maybe her dad was right. Maybe it was all a dream—or more like a nightmare.

"Code Blue. Room one nine four," the overhead speaker blared.

"Huh?" Lilith watched doctors and nurses race down the well-lit hallway. *Is it nighttime already?* She rubbed her eyes.

"Code Blue. Room one nine four," it repeated. *Code Blue* was never good. Lilith knew that much. She glanced at the board above Meghan's head. "One, nine, five," she mouthed.

Shouts, clattering, and beeping filled the next room—loud and frantic until it suddenly went silent. Lilith would have fixated on the quietness, but her gaze snagged on a faint glow behind the curtain next to her bed. Her pulse spiked and her wrist turned cold.

Swallowing her fear, she scooted to the edge of the bed, ready to pull the fabric aside.

"Ah!" Lilith flinched when someone grabbed her shoulder. "Flippin' toothpicks, Meghan!" she yelped, fists up in self-defense and her stepmom raised both hands in surrender. "Sorry, I—I just—ugh!" Lilith exhaled hard. "Wait—you *have* to see this," she said, grabbing Meghan's arm and dragging her toward the curtain.

"What? No!" Lilith complained to herself, peeking behind it with a frustrated groan.

The glow was gone.

"What?" Meghan asked, stretching her neck. "Did something happen?" she signed, drawing her head back.

"Never mind," Lilith muttered while signing.

"Are you sure you're okay?" Meghan asked, her brow creased with concern.

"Yeah. Dad's right. I should rest," she admitted, lying down and squeezing her eyes shut. That didn't help her sleep any faster, but at least she wouldn't have to answer a million questions—a strategy to avoid conversation she stuck to until they discharged her the next afternoon.

Lilith didn't bring up the boy again, even though he haunted her thoughts nonstop. *Who gets hit by a car, blacks out, and only wakes up with scraped knees?* That made zero sense. *She was probably losing her mind, wasn't she?*

"Pssst!" Amy, Lilith's six-year-old stepsister, hissed. She glanced at Meghan, who was still parking the car in their driveway, then turned back to Lilith. "Mom let me skip school to hang out with you today," she whispered excitedly, as if she'd pulled off the ultimate heist. Freckles dotted her face, and a sly grin said she was as mischievous as ever.

When Meghan opened the front door, Lilith quietly followed her inside, heading straight upstairs.

The house was oddly peaceful. Her unopened birthday gifts were still arranged around her room. She'd forgotten all about them.

Changing into pajamas, she shoved her stuffed penguin aside and settled on the bed, picking up the nearest gift to read its tag:

> *It's not every year you turn 12!*
> *Happy Birthday!*
> —*Uncle Zeek*

Lilith rolled her eyes. *Twelve? I'm fourteen.* She rolled her eyes, remembering Uncle Zeek's gift last year: fancy chocolates from the Noix store. The irony? Noix means "nuts" in French, and Lilith was allergic to nuts.

"Amyyyy!" Lilith called, her voice echoing through the house. "Wanna help me open my birthday gifts?"

Amy showed up in record time, panting. "Is that even a question?" she giggled, jumping onto the bed and grabbing the small package from Lilith's hands. "Oof! I'm glad Uncle Zeek isn't *my* uncle," Amy joked, twirling a finger beside her head. Then she tore open the box. "A... stone?" she said, lifting an eyebrow as she read the engraving: "*Keep on rocking.*"

"An actual stone? That's just—" Lilith struggled for words.

"Hi, girls," Meghan greeted, stepping in with a white plastic bag. "Lilith, the hospital returned these things you had with you when you were admitted," she signed one handed, handing it over with the other. "I'll be downstairs making dinner if either of you need me," she said, leaving.

Amy rummaged for another present, while Lilith peeked inside the plastic bag. "Ew," she muttered, pulling out her backpack. It was still soaked and smelled like sour socks. Lilith pinched the straps, carrying it to the corner of her room before dumping the rest of the plastic bag's contents on the bed.

"No way," Lilith mouthed, spotting an infinity pendant tangled up with her headphones and a squished snack bar. She might have stopped to sort through every impossible detail if panic hadn't punched through first: *what if the pendant goes insane and hurts Amy?*

"Uh-oh! I'm sorry," Amy said. Lilith spun around, heart leaping straight into her throat, certain her half-sister was talking about the necklace. But no. Amy held up a book whose cover dangled, almost detached from the spine. "I didn't mean to rip it! It was an accident, pinky swear!"

"It's fine," Lilith managed, her mind racing. She needed to protect Amy from the pendant and its craziness.

"Fine?" Amy asked, suspicious.

"Yeah. Totally fine. Why don't you grab a snack?" Lilith suggested, eyeing the door. "We can open more gifts tomorrow."

"Did you hit your head too hard? A snack? Dinner is almos—hmm... Never mind," Amy squinted, tiptoeing out of the room. Clearly, she sensed something was off but decided not to push her luck.

Lilith clutched the damaged book like a shield and crept toward the bed, heart pounding. She waited for the pendant to glow, but nothing happened. So she grabbed a ruler from her desk and poked it. Still nothing.

"Abracadabra?" she muttered, poking it several more times before setting the ruler aside.

Then she tossed random objects at it and also wiggled the sheets, but the pendant remained inert. She finally took a deep breath and, despite her brain fighting her actions, she picked it up, bracing for the worst—nothing. Lilith frowned and shook the glass, watching the white sand inside shift. "Wait, wasn't the sand blue? And why aren't you working?" she whispered.

"Who are you talking to, bud?" Nicholas asked from the doorway.

Lilith's heart slammed into her throat. *Dad?* Maybe she should've shown him the necklace and explained everything. Except he'd think she was delirious again. There was still no proof. It wasn't glowing, no sign of the boy. No, she couldn't tell him. Lilith forced a tight-lipped smile, turning to face him. "Just thinking out loud," she lied.

"Oh." Nicholas paused. "Hey, I'm sorry I couldn't drive you home earlier," he added, as though Lilith had been waiting for him. He was never around.

"It's okay," she said, rubbing her hands together nervously. The necklace slipped from her grasp, clattering on the floor. Her eyes nearly popped out of her head.

"Where did you get this?" Nicholas asked, crouching to pick it up. Lilith felt a surge of panic. *Was it going to explode? Trap him? Glow?*

"Uh... a girl at school gave it to me," she said slowly when nothing happened.

"That's..." He hesitated. "Huh! It reminds me of a necklace your mom had. It must be from a show or something."

"It does?" Lilith leaned in, curiosity sparking.

"I think so," he said with a shrug. "Here, let's see how it looks." Before she could protest, he looped it around her neck. "You look just like her," Nicholas said, his voice cracking.

He rarely spoke about her mother. Lilith stayed still, hoping he'd say more. Instead, he cleared his throat. "Anyway, I just came to tell you dinner's ready."

"Riiight," Lilith's voice wobbled. "I'm not hungry. Is it okay if I go to sleep instead?" She perched on the bed, feeling the weight of disappointment.

"Yeah, sure," Nicholas replied, stepping back. "Good night, bud." He flipped the light switch off and closed the door.

Lilith yanked the covers over her head and reached around for her mom's old stuffed penguin—the one that always made things feel a little better. Sadness bubbled up in her chest, but before the tears could come, she jerked back too quickly and bonked her back against the wall. *Was her wrist glowing?* Lilith's pulse raced. At least this time there was no car, no strange boy, and her arm wasn't stuck midair. *Was it all inside her head?*

She stood up and held her wrist closer to her eyes. The glow was so bright, she could actually read the words on Uncle Zeek's stone even with the lights off. Lilith pressed her fingers to the cold skin—it felt too real to be a dream. Slowly, she traced the pattern, her fingertip gliding along its edges. The moment she completed the loop, blue sparks burst to life, swirling around her in a sudden rush of light, swallowing the room.

"Wh—?" Lilith gasped, a wave of nausea rising in her throat. She flexed her fingers, trying to shake the strange tingling in her limbs as the blue light faded. "Where am I?"

CHAPTER THREE

NO RETREAT

L ilith's eyes took a moment to adjust to the brightness, yet her frown remained even after they did. *How was it sunny and hot?* It was dinnertime. Plus, spring had just started—it was supposed to be cloudy and rainy. Her heart pounded as she glanced around. Old colored ribbons tied to the rusty wire surrounding a soccer field fluttered in a light breeze. *A park?*

"Tem quatorze níveis no jogo! Eu encontrei dois níveis secretos! Zeus é o último chefe," a teenager squealed from the bleachers across the field, then high-fived the boy next to him.

"Fourteen levels in the game? Zeus?" Lilith muttered, knitting her brows even further. *Portuguese?* That couldn't be right. She'd never learned Portuguese. It made no sense.

A bird swooped so close it made Lilith duck, landing behind her and joining a dozen other pigeons around a picnic table. A white-haired man sat quietly there, pulling a handful of seeds from a crumpled bag and scattering them twice before rubbing his shoulder and wiping his sweaty face.

"Sir?" Lilith called, holding tightly to the pendant hanging around her neck, but he didn't answer. Then, the man clutched his chest. "Are you all right?" she cried, stepping forward.

The temperature of the pendant plummeted, exactly like the night of the accident. "Please, no," she whispered helplessly as the man slumped forward onto the table. Lilith shuddered. *Was he still breathing?* Her pulse hammered as she edged closer.

The man's chest rose and fell in ragged gasps—then stilled. Shimmering gold sand drifted from his body, pooling overhead. "Help," she tried to shout, but the word barely escaped as a strangled whisper.

The sparkling cloud twisted into a streak and sped up toward Lilith like a snake. "Ugh," she grunted, turning around, desperate to flee. She crashed against the fence and hit the ground with a jarring thud, burning her palms and knees. "No!" The shimmering trail pierced the air, shooting toward her. She raised her arms defensively, but the sand passed right through them and dove into the pendant around her neck as if they were made out of air.

Lilith lay there, too scared to move—even after the trail had finished trapping itself inside the pendant. Her clammy hands hovered above her face until her lungs demanded air.

"What in Fates' name are you doing?" a blond, fair-skinned boy growled. Lilith scrambled to her feet, stumbling backward. "Where's the rest of your team?" he demanded, furious. "Hannah, the soul. Now!" he shouted.

That was probably Lilith's cue to run, but instead she craned her neck, trying to see who he was talking to.

"Copy that!" A short girl with dark skin and two side buns dashed from behind him, sprinting past Lilith. Hannah made quick gestures with her hands, and a wing-shaped tattoo on her wrist glowed. Lilith peered at her own arm—the infinity symbol was still glowing there. At the bleachers, nobody seemed to notice any of this.

"Wha—" Lilith's jaw dropped as a translucent shape rose from the white-haired man's body.

Electric purple energy flickered between Hannah's hands. She spread her palms apart—almost like a reverse clap—forming a sphere of power. A purple portal flared in front of the man's ghostly form, and he stepped straight into it, disappearing from sight. Lilith's heart thundered. *A portal?* That was surreal. Then Hannah clapped her hands together, making the portal and the sphere vanish.

This has to be a dream. Lilith squeezed her eyes shut. But when she opened them, the sight remained.

"Done," Hannah announced. Her cloak fluttered behind her as she walked.

"What were you thinking?" the boy snapped, his jaw tight and blue eyes blazing. "That would've released another lost soul in the world!"

"There's no one else around, Adrien," came a new voice from above. Lilith tilted her head in time to see a tall, red-haired girl drop down with a heavy stomp. She looked older than the other two, her expression as stern as Nicholas's, although her freckles reminded Lilith of Amy.

"What do you mean, Kami?" Adrien asked, scowling.

"Wake up, wake up, wake up," Lilith chanted to herself.

"Wake up?" Adrien echoed, snapping his fingers. "Wait—you don't have a team, do you?" He glanced at the other girls, who exchanged wide-eyed looks. "How is that possible? It took me a week to move a single grain of Life Powder into my purifier," he said, shaking his head. "And you don't look like a Rogue, either," he mumbled.

"She's wearing *it* around her neck," Hannah interrupted, folding her arms. "No way this one is a Looper." Her tone dripped with sarcasm.

"I don't know who-the-looper-face is, but you have no business talking to me like that!" Lilith jutted her chin, trying to sound braver than she felt. "What in the world is going on—and who are you people?"

"Hold your sparks, Feisty!" Adrien said, raising his hands. He turned to the girl with the buns again. "Hannah, c'mon. Maybe she's not a Looper—yet," he added, voice softening. "But it sure seems like she's meant to be one. We need Professor Lewis."

"No way. We shouldn't even be here," Hannah muttered, glaring at Lilith. "I'm not getting in trouble over... *this*!"

"Kami?" Adrien pleaded, turning to the tall girl.

"Sorry, Hannah. I'm with Adrien on this one," Kami replied with a shrug.

"Fine, whatever." Hannah huffed. "When this goes wrong, remember: I was against running to Professor Lewis in the first place."

Adrien glanced at Lilith, his eyes locking onto hers. "So... it's up to you. If you really want to know what's happening, there's no better way than coming with us." He grabbed Hannah's hand, and Hannah took Kami's.

Lilith tilted her head. *What was happening?*

"So?" Adrien asked again, offering his free hand to Lilith.

That's when an infinity-shaped pendant sparkled under his sleeve, just like the one around her neck. If there was any chance she wasn't hallucinating, that pendant was the closest thing to an answer she had.

Lilith swallowed hard and took a breath like she was about to dive into an icy pool.

Well, she was definitely diving into something.

CHAPTER FOUR

IF MEMORIES COULD TALK

"I don't feel too good," Lilith mumbled after another flash of blue light. Her entire body tingled this time. She let go of Adrien's hand to cradle her head. They now stood in a wide hallway facing a large, ornately carved door with a golden-eyed owl knocker that Lilith could swear was watching her.

"Are you okay?" Adrien asked, fixing her with a level gaze. "Don't worry—you'll learn the tricks of teleporting. The spinning stops eventually, kind of. Then it's all blue lights, dramatic entrances, and getting places before anyone else even blinks," he said more quietly, casting a sideways glance at Hannah. "Miss Tough over there threw up on my sneakers the first week we trained," he added with a smirk.

Teleport. Lilith's head spun. *No way that was real.* She kept telling herself.

A distinct smell wafted through the door. Something like pine needles. It reminded her of the Christmas events Nicholas used to take her to when she was younger.

"Well?" Hannah called impatiently, tapping her foot.

"Yeah, yeah, calm down," Adrien replied. "Here we go," he said, lifting the creepy owl knocker and rapping it three times. The hallway echoed the sound before a man, roughly her dad's age, opened the door. He was nearly as tall as Kami, and his eyes were so dark they appeared plain black.

"Adrien?" the man said in a calm, deep voice. He tilted his head, short wavy hair falling to the side as he surveyed the others. "May I help you?"

"We hope so, Professor Lewis," Adrien answered with a nod. "I think we have a... situation."

Situation? Lilith thought. *More like craziness wrapped in insanity, but sure, let's call it a situation.* She pouted silently.

"Of course. Come in," Professor Lewis said, still puzzled as he pushed the door wider.

The space beyond was so tall Lilith couldn't see its ceiling. Endless shelves crowded with golden owls lined the walls, yet there were no ladders or stairs.

Lilith followed the group inside. They paused near a desk heaped with books of every size and color. On top of the nearest stack was a dark blue volume with silver lettering and some sort of seedy fruit engraved on its cover. Lilith glanced back, trying to make sense of all the small doors perched above the main entrance—although nobody else seemed intrigued.

"Hannah, Kami," Professor Lewis greeted the girl with the buns and the tall one, respectively. Then, he examined Lilith from head to toe—literally, since she had no shoes on. "I don't believe we've met yet," he said, intertwining his fingers in front of his chest. "I'm Professor Alfred Lewis. And you are...?"

Lilith's stomach twisted. *What had she gotten herself into? Who were these people?*

"L-Lilith," she stammered. "Lilith Agnes Fletcher, sir." She tried again.

"And she would be the... ahem... situation," Adrien spoke up, standing beside Lilith.

"Why is this new Looper a situation?" Professor Lewis asked, arching an eyebrow.

"Because technically, she's not a Looper?" Adrien rubbed his neck uncertainly. "But she's not a Rogue, either," he added.

"Hmm... I see." Professor Lewis nodded slowly and started walking toward a big table in the middle of the room. "Let's sit. I feel this may be a long conversation," he said, pulling out a chair.

Adrien followed suit, taking a seat on one of the white cushioned chairs. Lilith's toes pressed against the polished white floor while an uneasy heat spread through her chest. Fear pulsed through her mind, making her heart hammer so loud that she thought everyone could hear it. Maybe they could...since everyone was staring at her.

Could she teleport back home? Where were those freaky blue particles when she needed them? This had to be a weird, bad dream. Lilith's vision blurred as she lied to herself.

"Miss Fletcher?" Professor Lewis's voice broke through her haze, low and gentle. "Are you all right?"

"Huh? S-sorry." Lilith winced, tightening her scraped hands, still stinging from her frantic attempt to flee the swirling sand earlier. "I'm fine," she insisted, moving toward the table despite her buzzing head.

"So, as you are probably aware, Professor, we had a permission slip to gather Nyxhoppers today. But, well, we got a bit sidetracked," Adrien confessed, a lopsided grin creeping across his face.

"I see," Professor Lewis replied, leaning back as if this were a familiar refrain.

"Anyway," Adrien continued, "we stumbled on a Looper's call—by accident, of course—and found *her*." He pointed at Lilith. "She was collecting Life Powder. At first, I assumed she was an advanced apprentice, but then...she tried to run away, fell on the ground, and—"

"The soul almost escaped!" Hannah cut in. "Can you believe she didn't even have a Bridger with her? And who, in their right mind, wears a purifier around their neck?" she huffed.

Lilith sank lower in the suede chair as Adrien and Hannah argued over the details. *How could she mess up so badly?* Lilith had barely moved at the park.

"All right, all right," Professor Lewis said, raising both hands. "I think it's best if you all go outside while I speak with Miss Fletcher."

Hannah planted her fists on her hips, refusing to budge. "No way. I'm staying!" She glowered at Professor Lewis.

"That wasn't a request, obviously," Adrien teased, rolling his eyes before grabbing Hannah by her cloak and dragging her toward the exit. Kami followed, closing the door behind them.

"Miss Fletcher?" Professor Lewis called, settling back into his chair with a gentler expression.

"Y-yeah?" she croaked, nerves nearly paralyzing her.

"I'd like to help you. But first, I need to understand everything," he said, his voice calm and reassuring.

"That makes two of us," Lilith murmured, though it came out more like a question than a statement.

"Let's begin at the beginning, shall we?" he asked, nodding at her necklace. "Where'd you get that?"

"A boy?" Lilith intended to tell the whole story, but that was all she managed. *How could she possibly explain it all?* "Sorry," she said quietly, uncertain if he'd even heard.

"Huh," Professor Lewis scratched his chin. "Would you mind showing me what happened?"

"Showing?" Lilith repeated. "What does that even mean?"

"Well, sometimes I struggle to describe my memories, so it helps to simply focus and let them speak instead," he explained, resting his fingers on the table. "This table is... special. It'll help us. Place your wrist on that carving in front of you and think about what happened. That's all. How does that sound?"

Lilith studied the furniture. The table had twelve chairs, each with a carved symbol before them—an eye at the top, a semi-arch in the middle, like an umbrella, and a cross at the bottom.

"So?" Professor Lewis prompted gently.

"Sure," she said, putting her wrist against the carving.

"You're doing great. Just close your eyes and think about everything that happened. Don't worry about anything else," he encouraged.

Lilith nodded, inhaling deeply as she shut her eyes and replayed the events of her birthday evening—getting the cake, the car accident, that strange boy, then the hospital, going home, and how she touched the infinity symbol on her wrist and ended up at the park.

But how would reliving everything help Professor Lewis understand? she wondered, cracking one eye open, ready to ask him.

"Whoa," Lilith gasped. A projection of the park with every single detail she could remember was displayed above the table like a smoke hologram.

"And you can keep projecting even with your eyes open," Professor Lewis said with a wink. "Some people lose focus once they look around, but you are taking it like a pro."

Lilith exhaled shakily. Everything Nicholas had ever taught her since she was born said this was impossible—*but how could it be?* It was happening right in front of her!

"T-thank you?" she said, still staring at the projection before her. "Well, uh, the rest... you already know," Lilith pointed out when the hologram displayed Adrien knocking at Professor Lewis's office.

"That was very helpful, Lilith," he said with a smile. "You can lift your arm now."

The projection vanished as soon as Lilith moved her arm, though her eyes didn't move away, as if she expected the hologram to come back at any second.

"This is a gift, from one of Hephaestus's apprentices," he said, eyeing the furniture. "It translates memories into visible and audible form for anyone seated around it."

"So if everyone else was here, they would've seen my memories too?" Lilith asked, running a fingertip over the carved symbol.

"Yes, as long as they were seated in one of these chairs," Professor Lewis answered, gesturing to the matching carvings on each chair's armrest. "It's quite remarkable. The symbol represents Mnemosyne, the goddess of memory. And that's only a fraction of what this table can do," he finished with a grin.

Lilith wanted to ask more questions—her natural curiosity demanded it—but she held back. "I kind of wish this was a dream," she confided. "That boy... he died because of me. And that man at the park, too, right? I'm..." Lilith gulped. "I'm a killer. I don't even know how I became a killer." A flush of heat rose from her stomach to her face. She hunched over, throat tight. "I don't want to hurt anyone."

"Miss Fletcher, you're far from it," Professor Lewis reassured, standing to fetch a box of tissues and placing it beside her. "You did absolutely nothing wrong," he continued. "There's a reason gods have rules for activating gifts. This should never have happened to you without guidance."

"Then how do I undo it?" she demanded, gripping her shirt until her knuckles went white.

"There's nothing to undo," he said gently. "It was their time, Lilith. You only did what you were marked to do. If you were not there, another Looper would have collected their Life Powder."

"Marked?" She frowned, confused.

"Yes, by the Moirai—also known as the Fates," Professor Lewis replied.

"Like those three old ladies in the cartoon? The ones who share an eye, measure your life, and cut a thread when you're done?" Lilith pressed her fingertips to her temples. It was as though someone poured cement into her brain, grinding her thoughts to a halt.

"Sort of. They're indeed three sister goddesses. But they don't share an eye, they share visions. And, yes, their purpose is to guide humans into and out of life," he explained.

"You're saying this is about gods? Like, for real?" Her eyebrows shot up. She'd never been religious. The idea seemed ridiculous—just like fairy tales or aliens.

"Specifically the Olympian gods," he said with a neutral expression. "The Fates gifted Loopers," Professor Lewis pointed at Lilith, "and I, for example, was gifted by Athena," he added, pushing up his sleeve to show a small black owl tattoo. "All Gifted are guided to an Academy to learn how to use their powers."

Lilith swallowed. "And how exactly do Loopers use their gift?" The question came out slow. Not because she couldn't guess the answer, but because she didn't want to believe it.

Professor Lewis took a moment, carefully forming his response. "Think of humans as made up of flesh, soul, and fuel," he said. "Flesh is the body." He raised one hand. "The soul is our personality, choices, and memories." He lifted the other. "And the fuel is Life Powder, which ignites them and ties the flesh and soul together." He brought his hands together.

Lilith curled her toes, her chin trembling. Professor Lewis paused and waved his hands slowly. Four small fire orbs rose from the ground and circled around them, emitting a comfortable warmth.

"Need a break?" he asked softly.

She shook her head. "I need answers."

"All right," he said with a nod. "Life Powder powers the flesh. And Loopers use purifiers to collect, store, recycle, and give this fuel. In short, Loopers maintain cosmic order and balance," he explained as if everything he said made complete sense.

"So, you *are* saying I'm some kind of... grim reaper?" Lilith shook her head. "They can't force me to kill people! That's not right!" she shouted.

"You are right. Being marked doesn't mean you must accept a gift, Miss Fletcher, but—" he hesitated.

"But I accepted mine when that boy asked me. Didn't I?" She pressed her lips together.

He sighed. "Yes, you and the pendant are bound now. If you don't learn to use it, you put yourself—and others around you—in danger."

"That's not fair!" she roared, shoving her chair back so hard it toppled. Lilith's voice cracked with desperation. "I didn't mean to accept it—I don't want to kill anybody!" She broke, the vein on her forehead throbbing. "You better take this gift back or I'll get rid of this pendant, burn it to ashes!"

"If I could free you, I would," Professor Lewis said, trying to comfort her, stepping closer. "But if that purifier breaks—and that's a big 'if,' since it's a deity tool—you would die along with it," he said. "It's linked to your own Life Powder. And that's why not learning to control it is even more dangerous than you can possibly imagine."

Lilith felt like her lungs were collapsing under the weight of her shock. She sank onto the floor without a word.

"Miss Fletcher?" Professor Lewis crouched beside her. "Lilith?"

But she couldn't answer. Her thoughts crashed into each other in a frenzied storm of confusion and fear. The warmth in the room only deepened the chill in her chest as she stared at the white floor, her mind unable to process it all.

CHAPTER FIVE

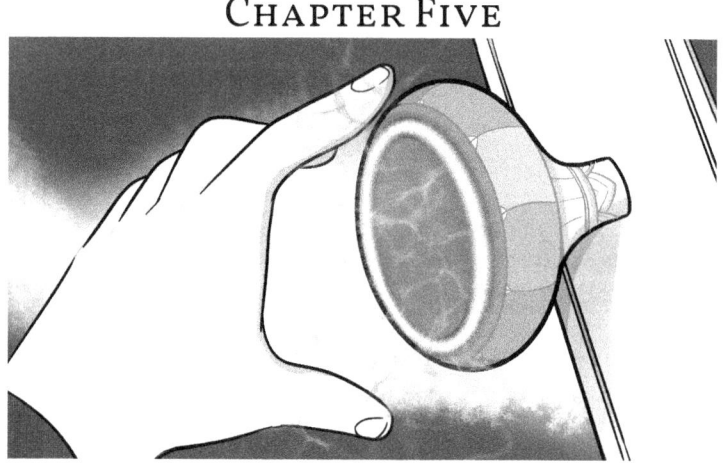

INTO THE UNKNOWN

After what felt like an eternity of silence, Professor Lewis gently tapped the floor. "I know this is overwhelming, but you're not alone. We'll guide you every step of the way."

Lilith looked up, meeting his eyes. The sincerity in his gaze offered a flicker of hope amid the chaos. "I... I don't know if I can do this," she whispered, voice trembling.

"You can," he replied firmly. "It'll take time, and it won't be easy, but you have the strength. You were gifted by the Fates for a reason. Give it time."

She drew a long breath, letting his words sink in. Then, she nodded slowly. "Okay," she said softly. "I'll try."

"Good. That's all we ask—one step at a time." Professor Lewis smiled, rising to his feet and helping her up.

After righting the fallen chair so Lilith could sit, he opened a small wooden cabinet near the right wall. Lilith stretched her neck to see inside—it was empty. The professor glanced around and used a short bamboo stick to scribble something on a piece of tanned paper. Then he clipped the note to a string inside the cabinet, gave it a gentle tug, and closed the small door.

"We'll sort this out," he said. "This is highly unusual, but we'll figure it out. For now you need rest. Let's get you settled."

A clunky noise echoed from the cabinet. Professor Lewis turned, opened the little door again, and revealed a pair of black shoes that had appeared as if by magic. Smiling, he walked over and held them out to Lilith.

"Here. You'll need these," he said.

"Shoes?" Lilith asked, reaching for the shiny flats.

"Yes," he assured her. "We'll get you the rest of your things soon. And we'll give you a uniform to wear while you stay here with us."

"For how long?" she asked softly.

"Unfortunately, my answer would be indefinite," he said gently.

"Indefinite," Lilith echoed under her breath, sliding the oversized shoes onto her feet. They didn't fit at all, which was ironically similar to how Lilith had always felt. *Did that feeling exist because she was "marked" for this? Was she supposed to be someone else all her life?*

"Please, think of staying as an opportunity. I don't want to frighten you," Professor Lewis went on. "Here you can learn to control your gifts without risking anyone's life, including yours. The Academy has a protection spell that prevents you from removing Life Powder from humans. In other words, safe grounds. And during your first-year training, you'll only practice on plants and simulators—keeping everyone safe and giving you time to process it all."

Lilith gave a tight nod. The last thing she wanted was to harm anyone else—again. But the word anyone snagged in her mind and twisted into faces. *Amy. Meghan. Dad.* "Okay, but... what about my sister? And Meghan, and Dad? Won't they freak out if I'm not in bed when they wake up?"

"They'll be fine. The Academy will bless them with the veil of illusion, so their memories will be... shifted a bit," Professor Lewis said. Lilith raised an index finger, paused, then lowered it again. At this point, it was easier to just accept what he said than to question it. He smiled softly. "Sorry, I didn't explain it properly. We'll make them believe you're studying abroad. You can still visit them on designated days—once we're sure you're prepared. And you're allowed phones or other devices to keep in touch outside class hours."

"So... bent memories. Right." Lilith blinked. Then, her eyes widened as she looked down at her feet. *Are my shoes shrinking?*

"Comfortable?" Professor Lewis asked, eyeing the shoes.

"They're... a perfect fit," she said, putting weight on her back foot, checking if the size would change again.

"It's remarkable how sometimes, where we are can shape who we become," he mused. "Before we assign your room, could I see your purifier for a moment?" Professor Lewis extended one hand, holding a small leather book in the other.

"You can keep it for all I care," Lilith said with a pout.

The book he held had a white infinity symbol on the cover, but between the pages inside there was an infinity-shaped slot where Professor Lewis placed her purifier. *A fake book.*

"This is an emergency refiller for Loopers," he explained. "Its ink is made of Life Powder." He closed the cover over the pendant. "Yours is nearly empty, and outside the Academy, it could accidentally draw Life Powder from nearby humans. But now you'll have enough to stay safe and to practice with while you learn." He reopened the cover. The pages around the slot were blank this time, but the pendant was nearly full of sand.

Lilith drew a long breath before reaching for the necklace. Professor Lewis held it out to her, and she took it carefully, its weight settling in her palm. *How could something so little control life and death?*

The scrape of Professor Lewis's chair pulled her back. He stood and gestured toward the door. "Now let's get you settled."

"Professor Lewis?" Lilith asked, gripping the pendant in her fist.

"Yes?" He paused by the door.

"The day of the accident... the purifier was empty," she said, and he nodded. "So if that boy hadn't made me the pendant's owner, it would've sucked my Life Powder instead of his?"

"Yes," Professor Lewis said quietly. "He made himself the target. I believe he knew what he was doing."

"Why would he do that?" Lilith murmured, frowning.

"That I can't say." His mouth formed a thin line.

"Thanks," she said, inhaling deeply. "Oh—one more question?"

"As many as you have."

"How can a purifier run out of powder? Why was it so empty?"

"Mmm," Professor Lewis sighed. "The most common ways include using Life Powder in battle and not calling it back, or giving too much of it without taking any in return. Realistically speaking, there are many possibilities."

"Do you think that he was trying to help me?" Lilith asked, hope and confusion warring in her voice.

"Sometimes things are too blurry to see without the right lens," he said cryptically.

"You talk funny," she said, raising an eyebrow. "So, what's next?" she asked, putting on her bravery coat.

"Let's find your room," Professor Lewis replied, heading to the door.

"Okay." Lilith put the pendant around her neck and followed him into the hall.

There was no sign of Adrien, Hannah, and Kami—*they had probably gotten tired of waiting*. Lilith stared at the floor quietly as they advanced, fighting lingering questions: *who was that boy? Why did he give her his pendant?*

"This is the Academy's main entrance," Professor Lewis said after a while, gesturing to his right.

Lilith's eyes wandered in awe as she stepped into the room. It was vast and majestic, with slender columns stretching toward a high ceiling. At the center, a fountain shimmered under soft light. Carvings of ancient gods and forgotten legends lined the walls, their symbols woven into the stone like secrets. At the far end, two enormous double doors towered before her, each etched with breathtaking detail—wide enough to fit three or four of her bedrooms side by side.

The floor shifted beneath her feet. It was subtle—barely a sway—but definitely moving. The polished white stone gleamed under the ambient light, smooth as glass. In the center, a magnificent blue compass rested, its edges traced with delicate gold lines. The needle stayed fixed on north, yet the entire disc spun slowly beneath it, as if caught in a graceful dance of stars.

"Aparctias, Apeliotes, Notos, and Zephyrus," Lilith read aloud. "North, East, South, and West? Wait—how do I even know this?"

"Loopers have many skills besides powder manipulation," Professor Lewis said, stepping closer. "One of them is the power of communication. Any language you encountered in your first fourteen years awakens once your mark is activated. You learn new ones faster, too."

"So... the kids at the park really were speaking... Portuguese?" she guessed.

"Yes," he answered. "And you probably already know many more languages and might not have realized yet." He turned, gesturing toward the columns lining the room, each holding a statue at its center. "That's Hestia, Hephaestus, Demeter, Poseidon, Dionysus, Artemis, Zeus..."

Lilith instantly forgot most of the names, but she counted fourteen statues in all. She also took note of the ones she recognized: Poseidon, with his iconic trident, and Dionysus, who she was pretty sure was the god of grapes.

Sparkling fragments dotting the floor around the compass glowed with an ethereal light. "What is that?"

"Star fragments," Professor Lewis said. "Filled with frozen wishes."

How could fragments from a hot ball of gas be infused into the floor? Lilith crouched, examining one of the sparkling spots up close. "Frozen wishes?" she mouthed in disbelief.

"When people wish on shooting stars for selfish or harmful ends, those wishes can freeze and fall as fragments." Lilith marveled at the idea—*frozen wishes scattered like cosmic breadcrumbs.* "Anyway, that door straight ahead leads to the Oracle Room," he continued, pointing at the door below the double staircase. "You'll get your room number there."

"Oracles? Oracles give answers, right? Like what to do to get rid of this whole gift thing?" Lilith blurted, heart flickering with hope.

"In theory, maybe. But Oracles are tricky. They don't answer what you want to know. They follow their own agenda. Sometimes they can also tell you nothing at all. I was told they share what you are supposed to know. It's hard to explain, you'll see... I'll wait here," he added, leaning against the wall. "One way or another, I hope you find what you're after."

"Humph," Lilith grumbled, squaring her shoulders as she approached the gleaming white door with its gold frame. She was determined to get real answers this time.

Just as she stepped forward, thin teal veins of light snaked across the wood. They crept to the edges, filling carved symbols with a glow like living ink. One symbol caught her eye—an infinity shape, identical to the mark on her wrist.

Here goes nothing. She reached for the round golden knob, its edges etched with teal. Before her fingers touched it, a voice—no, more like a presence—brushed past her ear, whispering words that sent icy tingles down her spine.

"Beware of your traveled soul—
Though Hades's threads are closest,
Your room is Pi-Theta, under Zeus Wing.
The kiss of a flower will make you bloom,
For the battles ahead and the secrets behind."

The whisper shifted, now curling into her other ear.

"You'll meet the ones you need at 3:09 PM tomorrow,
Beneath the Phaunos Tree."

A jolt of static snapped at her fingertips. "Ow!" she gasped, jerking her hand back.

Teal smoke coiled from her fingers, then vanished into the air. Every word of the message had branded itself into her memory—clearer than any textbook. Her brow furrowed at the fading glow of the door, heart racing.

"Traveled soul? Secrets?" she whispered, the words catching on her breath like echoes.

"I guess you weren't invited in today, then. Most people aren't," Professor Lewis called out from afar, shifting his weight against the doorframe. "Did you get the answers you wanted?"

"I didn't even get to ask a question," she replied, crossing her arms in front of her chest. "But I got a room in Zeus Wing. Pi-Theta?"

"Zeus?" Professor Lewis said thoughtfully. "It's been a while since we placed a Looper in any wing other than Hades. That is... interesting." He clapped his hands once. "Well, let's get you a map," he announced, walking to the fountain at the center of the lobby, in front of the Oracle's door.

Curious, Lilith leaned in to peer at the water. Spouts around the fountain's base started pumping water upward in a rhythmic pattern. The water rose steadily, then defied gravity and hung in midair.

Lilith stepped back.

Instead of splashing everywhere, the water rose into intricate walls, stairs, and floors—a shimmering, fluid blueprint. Lilith stood rooted to the spot as the liquid shaped itself into an elongated building with majestic columns, six broad steps at its entrance, and a domed structure at the top. *A map.*

"This is the visitor's map for the Academy," Professor Lewis said. "Classrooms, dining hall, basic rooms." He pointed to a carving of a wing on the marble base. "Go ahead and place your wrist here."

"Professor Lewis, that wing symbol—didn't Hannah have the same one?" Lilith asked.

"Yes, it's the mark from Hermes," he confirmed. "He's the god of travelers, but he does more than that—like guiding souls to the underworld and influencing the earthly economy. You might've seen him in movies with winged sandals."

"So Hannah was guiding that man's soul to the underworld," Lilith assumed, and he nodded in response.

As soon as Lilith rested her wrist on the carving, the water in the fountain began to fizz. She squeezed her eyes shut, bracing for pain—but this time, none came.

Curiosity won out, and she slowly reopened them.

The bubbling slowed, revealing a piece of paper at the fountain's bottom. Lilith picked it up. It felt dry, except for a wet circle in the center. When she held her wrist over the circle, the water spread, painting a map across the blank page.

"You're a natural," Professor Lewis teased. "This guide will show you the way to the dining room when it's mealtime, or to a classroom, and so on. If you want a specific location, just place your wrist on the map and think about it."

"Everything's getting crazier by the minute," Lilith muttered, tracing her finger from the entrance hall to a labeled Pegasi camp. *Flying horses?* She blinked twice before glancing up at Professor Lewis.

"You haven't seen half of it," he said with a wink. "Just don't forget to water your map now and then. You wouldn't want it drying out."

"Water. The map?" Lilith blinked, tilting her head.

"A spoonful a week should do," he replied, as if that were the most ordinary thing in the world.

"Okay..." she said slowly, staring at the tanned parchment in her hands and half-expecting a leaf to sprout if she poured water on it.

"Should we give it a try?" he asked.

"I guess?" Lilith said, refocusing. "Zeus Wing, Pi-Theta," she said aloud. The map reacted instantly, showing the path from the lobby to her new room.

"You don't have to say it out loud," Professor Lewis said with a chuckle, and Lilith gave a sheepish grin.

She glanced back at the Oracle Room. The stairs curving above it branched off to different corridors. It was exactly like the map showed.

"For reference," Professor Lewis continued, "classrooms on more advanced classes are upstairs. The right hallway leads to the dining room, and the left to the common hall." He began walking again while adjusting his sleeve slightly.

"Professor, how come my Fates' mark turns on and off with the glowing but yours is just there—black?" she asked.

"That's a good question," he replied. "Our marks glow when we are actively using our gift. Over time, the magic wears into our skin, and it becomes a permanent mark. The glow still turns on and off, though."

They passed into a long corridor that seemed to thrum with magic. The dark mustard wallpaper was richly textured, and the ambient light cast shifting shadows across the walls.

"Are those... moving?" Lilith came a bit closer to Professor Lewis.

"Yes. This is the Wisdom Hall," Professor Lewis said. "It's fueled by the Oracles to display past events relevant to people walking through. Can you recognize this scene?" He pointed to their right.

Lilith checked without straying too far from him. Ink-like drawings formed three women. The first spun a wheel, the second measured string, and the third cut it. *The Fates?* Lilith wondered as the third woman on the wall gazed at Earth, falling in love with a mortal.

"Those are the Fates, right?" she guessed. "Is that guy..." she asked, pointing at the forging figure crafting pendants from shattered tools. "He... Hefa—sorry, I can't pronounce it. The god connected to that memory table in your office. The one who makes weapons and stuff," she mumbled.

"Hephaestus," Professor Lewis supplied. "And yes, that's correct."

Lilith squinted at a person lurking behind Hephaestus's counter. "Who's that?"

"Hm..." Professor Lewis stepped up, studying the image. "I'm not sure." He paused, as though memorizing the scene.

They continued walking, passing more murals as Professor Lewis spoke about the three gods who founded the Academy and something about checking the level of her skills. Lilith tried to listen, but her attention kept straying to the stories unraveling across the wall.

By the time they stepped out of the Wisdom Hall and into an elegant, echoing chamber, Lilith realized she barely heard a word he'd said.

"Sorry—what did you say?" she asked, shaking her head and trying to focus. *Less looking, more listening,* she scolded herself.

"I said we're almost there," Professor Lewis repeated as they arrived at an indoor garden labeled *DIPLOMATIC TERRACE.* Carved symbols of gods adorned the columns, though Lilith only recognized two of the symbols: Hermes's wing and Athena's owl. Flowers thrived everywhere, and the air was so crisp that Lilith's lungs nearly burst with relief.

"Here," Professor Lewis said as they reached a chamber with no visible exit.

Before them stood three towering pairs of statues shaped like wings. Each pair flanked a section of the wall, silent and still like ancient guardians.

"Zeus, Poseidon, and Hades," he explained, pointing to the carved symbols above each set—lightning bolt, trident, and a strange, jagged key. "The wings only open for students assigned to them—and for staff, of course."

"So... Zeus is in there?" Lilith asked, knees suddenly weak at the thought of meeting an actual god in person.

CHAPTER SIX

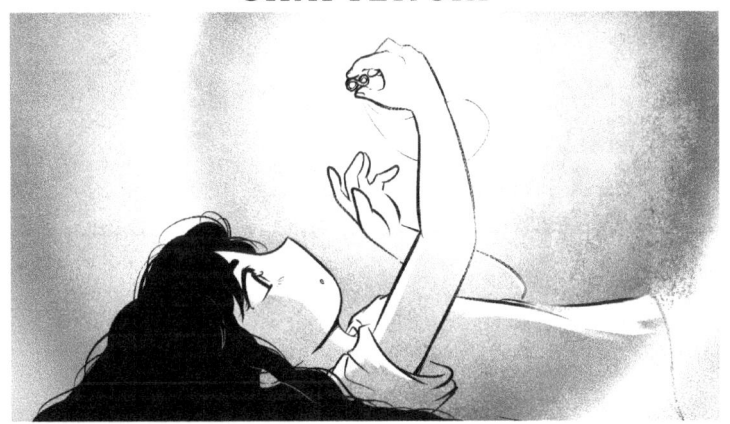

BLENDING WITH THE CLOUDS

A s Lilith stood before the golden pair of wings, watching them slowly spread open, she couldn't help but wonder—*could Zeus fix this mess? Unbind her? He was a god, after all.*

"Oh, Miss Fletcher," Professor Lewis said with a soft chuckle, snapping her out of the thought. "The gods don't come here. They haven't set foot on Academy grounds for centuries. They aren't allowed. It keeps their secrets hidden from one another."

He motioned toward the doorway. "Let's get you settled."

Lilith stepped through—and stopped short. The ceiling had vanished. Sunlight spilled over her face, warm and real, while clouds drifted across a stretch of open blue above her. Behind her, the doorway still stood inside the wings chamber. In front of her, a courtyard stretched wide and sky-soaked. Wide. Bright. Untamed.

It couldn't have been more than a few hours since Nicholas had turned off her bedroom light and told her good night. It had to be the middle of the night by now. Yet here, the sun was already tilting toward the horizon, because apparently even the sky refused to make sense there.

"Whoa!" She flinched when a boy summoned lightning with a flick of his wrist, the crackle momentarily filling her ears.

"Don't worry. He's just training," Professor Lewis assured her. "Come, the Pi area's this way." He led her deeper into the courtyard, and her senses went into overdrive.

A girl beside a white beanbag juggled four electric orbs without letting a single one wobble, while others chatted and walked around as sparks, gusts, and tiny flashes of light flickered around them. Every corner teemed with strange sights and sounds, flooding Lilith with awe and apprehension.

Eventually, they reached an oval common area draped with gold curtains, with twelve identical doors arranged in perfect symmetry.

"Welcome to the Pi common area," Professor Lewis said, gesturing around. Then, he pointed to a door marked with a Theta symbol. "That's your new room."

Her eyes moved across the doors, each etched with a different symbol. For a change, she recognized them all—thank goodness for math class.

"Get some rest," he added. "As I mentioned, you'll need energy for the assessment tomorrow."

"Uh?" Lilith turned to Professor Lewis. *When had he said anything about assessments? Wait... probably in Wisdom Hall, when the ink on the walls kept shifting from gods to monsters to threads, and she had kept nodding even though his words had blurred into a distant hum.* She was regretting that now.

"No need to worry. It's just to assign you to the correct classes," he said with a smile. "And if you need anything, let me know." He rummaged through his jacket pockets—more than she cared to count—before producing a weird slim black pen. "This is a waterbub. Fill it with water, write a message on your map, and add the recipient's name. They'll receive it on theirs, including me." Lilith nodded. "I've got a meeting now, but I'll keep an eye on my map. And send the head girl to help you tomorrow." He winked, heading off.

"Professor?" she called. "I—I don't have a key."

"You are the key," he replied, raising his marked wrist. "And—Miss Fletcher," he added, looking over his shoulder by the archway, "you'll be fine."

Lilith murmured, "Theta," under her breath as she approached the door. Her finger slid over the cool metal, tracing the symbol—an oval bisected by a thin line—before reaching the handle. As she turned the knob, the infinity symbol on her wrist pulsed with light, and the door clicked open.

She was *literally* the key. *Of course she was.*

With a sigh, she stepped into her new quarters. It was a double room with two canopy beds, each decked in gold drapery tied to corner poles.

Did she have a roommate? Lilith wondered, scanning the space. On the left side, the room appeared untouched. On the other, three neatly folded uniforms and a basket with a small card rested on the bed. "*Lilith A. Fletcher,*" she read aloud before sinking beside them—*how did they get all of that done so fast?* The mattress cushioned her aching muscles, and she exhaled, exhaustion settling in like never before.

She closed her eyes, her thoughts swirling. A secret world she'd never known, suddenly laid bare. Part of her was oddly excited—if only it didn't involve "collecting Life Powder" from people. After a deep breath, she gazed at the cottony-looking ceiling, her legs still dangling off the bed.

Could she just return this so-called "gift"? The thought took root, spreading fast. *What if she spoke to the Fates—asked them to take it back?* She considered messaging Professor Lewis to see if that was even possible, but before she could, sleep pulled her under.

Knock, knock, knock!

"I'm coming, Dad!" Lilith yawned, stretching her arms overhead.

She blinked, still half-dazed. What a bizarre, vivid dream—*Loopers, Life Powder, a magical Academy.* She rubbed her eyes, chuckling at the absurdity.

Bang, bang, bang!

"Fletcher? Professor Lewis sent me to fetch ya!" came a high, sing-song voice.

Lilith's heart lurched. *It was all real.*

"You have your very own personal guide for the assessment today."

Oh, right—the assessment. Lilith bolted upright. "Coming!" she yelled, hurriedly changing into one of the uniforms.

Lilith struggled to knot the tie and tossed it back on the bed. She barely knew how to tie a bow when wrapping a gift, let alone a proper tie. Tugging on her jacket and stuffing the map and waterbub in a pocket, she rushed to the door. "Sorry," she said, attempting to smooth her gray skirt. "I, uh, wasn't ready yet."

"That's on me. I didn't set your sunrise yet... Anyway, I'm Kallista Lambros, but everyone calls me Kalli—head girl for Zeus Wing, at your service." She offered a playful bow. Her hair was two-toned, a vibrant blue at the roots that faded into an aqua-icy hue. Loose French braids framed her face, making it look like dancing blue flames.

"Hi," Lilith replied shyly. "I'm Lilith Fletcher. Nice to meet you."

Kallista stood half a head taller and seemed a little older, too—maybe because of the makeup. She wore a spotless uniform with five pins over the Academy logo: a crystal pin at the top featuring a bow and arrow, two gold pins (a crescent moon and a tree), two silver pins (a leaf and a sparkly hand), and a bronze pin depicting a half-wolf, half-human head.

Noticing Lilith's gaze on her pins, Kallista added, "Nice to meet you, too! These?" she touched the pins on her chest. "They're skill badges. You'll get some after your assessment today."

"Got it," Lilith replied.

"Okay! Let's grab food first, shall we?" Without waiting for an answer, Kallista spun around and dashed out of the Pi area.

Lilith jogged to keep pace as students bustled past, all in gray bottoms with white shirts beneath dark jackets and shiny black shoes.

"You forgot your tie?" Kallista asked, raising an eyebrow. "They're mandatory. Also, it helps identify your wing: blue with gold for Zeus, aqua with copper for Poseidon, and black with silver for Hades."

"Sorry," Lilith mumbled, cheeks warming.

Kallista waved a hand dismissively. "It's your first day. You're fine. I heard you had a really bumpy introduction to the Academy too," she said with a smile.

They walked on, Kallista chatting a mile a minute until they reached a dining hall large enough to fit at least eight of Lilith's houses. Three concentric rings of tables filled the space: an outer ring of eight curved tables, a middle ring of four, and an inner ring of two slightly raised semicircles. The place was filled with food of all kinds. The table on their right had fruits and cereals, while the one on their left was piled with waffles, pancakes, toast, eggs, and bacon.

"What do you feel like eating?" Kallista asked. "You can sit anywhere the food speaks to you, except for the teachers' tables." She nodded toward the two elevated central tables.

Lilith said nothing, too captivated by the globe floating overhead—a dark teal sphere wrapped in golden continents. Sparkles orbited around it, reminding her of the Mnemosyne table's hologram.

"That's Earth," Kallista explained, following Lilith's curious gaze—she didn't miss much. "The sparkles around it are the Olympian Schools in real time. It's our global tracker."

"Schools? Plural?" Lilith echoed, her jaw dropping.

Kallista nodded. "Yeah, a huge crisis almost happened ages ago, so they created the Owens Tracking System—O.T.S. for short. Helps keep watch." She pointed at a spot on the globe's upper left. "We're the blue sparkle above Europe. The other schools appear gold."

"So... we're *flying*?" Lilith managed, disbelief thick in her voice.

Kallista laughed, steering Lilith toward an empty spot at the table on their left. With a flick of her fingers, a worn map whooshed into her grasp. The bow-and-arrow mark on her wrist glowed as water spread across the parchment, revealing a detailed landscape. It mirrored the Academy's main structure from the fountain map, but included more—a lake, waterfalls, and even a river.

"How is that possible?" Lilith asked, tracing the sky-like outline.

"It's cool, right? We're hidden by a ring of clouds. The unmarked people down on Earth think it's just storms." Kallista winked. "Trust me—some of the other school locations are even wilder. I once had an extracurricular class under the ocean and another on the back of a giant turtle!" She grinned, leaving Lilith's mind spinning with questions.

A waterfall midair? Where did the water even go—or where did it come from? Lilith tried to slow her brain down, but apparently it was having trouble applying logic to a place that defied reality.

"Anyway, we don't want you to be late. Dig in!" Kallista urged, reaching for a stack of moon-shaped waffles and waving her hand, making the map disappear into thin air.

Lilith slowly stacked a few pancakes onto her plate, but the food might as well have been dust—she could barely taste anything. She had finally jumped off the *this makes no sense train*, only to land straight in the *I can't do this pit*. Her nerves churned, twisting like an unraveling thread.

Kallista must have noticed, because she gave Lilith a look. "Don't worry. The assessment's pretty chill," she said, her tone light.

Lilith inhaled slowly, then gave a small nod.

She could do this, right? She had to—at least until she found a way back home.

CHAPTER SEVEN

WHAT ABOUT THE DESKS?

E ach step down the hallway grew heavier as they neared the assessment room. Uncertainty pressed against Lilith's chest.

"Ready?" Kallista asked brightly, pointing at the wooden door. Lilith just shrugged. "Do you mind if I ask why you're wearing your purifier around your neck?"

"Hannah mentioned something about me wearing it wrong," Lilith replied, tugging the pendant as if checking it was still there. "Honestly? I'm not sure what I'm supposed to do with it."

"Oh, I can help. May I?" Kallista asked.

"Sure." Lilith shrugged.

Kallista circled around Lilith and unclasped the necklace. "Give me your left wrist." She wrapped the string around Lilith's wrist three times before fastening it over the spot where the infinity symbol had glowed earlier. "There, all set! I'll see you inside," she added, propping the door open.

"You're not coming?" A fresh wave of dread twisted inside Lilith.

"Oh, I figured you knew! I have to go through the other door to join the staff. But don't worry, I'll be there in a sec, and it's just a straight shot for you now."

"Got it," Lilith said, summoning every ounce of courage and stepping through the door. "I'll see you soon then."

The blinding light at the corridor's end loomed ahead, almost as intimidating as the soft thud of the door closing behind her. Lilith squared her shoulders—*everything would be fine once she figured out how to return this so-called gift to the Fates.*

"Crispy crackers!" She'd totally forgotten to ask Professor Lewis how to contact the Fates! Now she'd have to wait until after the assessment. Lilith shook her head. No use dwelling on it—not that she would for long. Her brain short-circuited the second the corridor ended. Rows of empty seats towered around a central arena. *A stadium?*

Four people sat behind a long desk on a raised platform, while Professor Lewis waited below near the arena floor. That was it—five people other than her in that humongous place, and they would all be studying her every move along with Kallista very soon. A lump formed in Lilith's throat, and a cold prickle raced down her arms as Professor Lewis walked in her direction. Why did her body always freeze up when she got nervous? When they'd said assessment, she'd pictured multiple-choice questions, not a gladiator showdown.

I'm so going to get squashed. Lilith wiped her sweaty palms—even though she knew they'd be wet again in the next five seconds.

"Welcome, Miss Fletcher. I'm hoping you got some rest?" Professor Lewis said gently. "This should be easy. Today is not about doing things right or wrong, just about trying them so we can see what you can do."

"Sure," she muttered. Like anything was ever "easy" for her.

"To prove I'm telling the truth," Professor Lewis continued, extending his palm to reveal a Looper's crystal pin, "you've already earned a badge just for showing up." He winked.

"Thanks," she said, taking the pin and fastening it just above the crest on her jacket. It resembled Kallista's crystal pin, except instead of a bow and arrow, it bore an infinity symbol.

"Remember to breathe, Miss Fletcher," Professor Lewis said. "We only want to place you in the right classes." Although Lilith could tell he meant well, it didn't really calm her down. Not one bit.

"Shall we begin?" A deep voice boomed across the arena.

Lilith lifted her gaze. One of the people sitting behind the long desk on the platform—a man with short, silvery hair and a neatly trimmed beard—laced his fingers together.. He looked like the kind of person who would make Amy bolt straight under a blanket. Lilith would never admit it, but if she had one right there, she might have done the same.

"Certainly, Ezra," Professor Lewis responded, making his way up there to take a seat beside him. Kallista arrived right after, greeting them all before taking a seat too.

A dizzy wave hit Lilith when all eyes turned toward her. *So this is what being on a TV show feels like,* she thought.

"Welcome to A.M.A., formally known as the Aeternitas Motus Academy, Miss Fletcher," the silver-haired man announced. "I'm Principal Stewart." Then his tone shifted from warm to matter-of-fact. "Today's tasks will gauge your abilities so we can place you in the appropriate classes. Each one will test a different skill and each task comes with a time limit." He paused, letting that sink in before he continued. "We're here to assess and guide you," he added, voice softening. "Now, please step onto that circle." He gestured toward the middle of the arena floor.

"For your first task, we'll assess your teleportation level," Principal Stewart said, his voice steady. "Instructions will appear below." He gestured to the front panel of the long desk where the professors sat. Golden instructions shimmered across the desk's midnight-stone front panel, bright enough for Lilith to read from the arena floor. "Feel free to ask questions if anything is unclear. Do you understand?" Lilith gave a quick nod but failed to form actual words. "Good," he continued, tapping a floating hourglass beside him as golden grains of sand began to fall—marking the start of her time.

The symbols finished forming quickly on the black granite. Lilith squinted, trying to make sense of the display. A Looper's badge hovered over five empty skill slots in the center of the display, right below where Principal Stewart sat. Then, under the slots, a sequence of steps appeared from left to right: stand in the white circle, focus on the blue circle a few feet away, visualize teleportation, and a hazy success with swirling particles.

Lilith had already teleported to a park. *Not just any park, either. One in another country.* Teleporting from the white circle to the blue one didn't sound too hard, although she wasn't looking forward to the nausea or tingles. Lilith inhaled deeply, then traced over the purifier's shape. But nothing happened. She shook it off before trying again. Then she repeated the gesture—eyes open, eyes closed, focusing on the circle, then her wrist, and even trying to run as if momentum might help her teleport. Still nothing.

How was she supposed to do the rest of that test if she couldn't even do something she had already done? Lilith shot a worried glance at the hourglass—more than two-thirds of the sand was gone. Panic gripped her chest, the same way it had months ago when she got caught sneaking into Dad's closet for pictures of her mom.

She had to be doing something wrong. But what? *The only thing that had changed from before was...* She bit her lip. *If Hannah were here, she'd probably leap into the arena and growl at me.* Lilith thought as she unfastened the purifier from her wrist and looped it back around her neck.

"What are you doing, child?" Principal Stewart's voice echoed around the arena.

Lilith stiffened under his glare. "I, uh, I don't—I didn't..." she stammered.

"Let the girl be," Professor Lewis interjected. "Experimenting is part of learning."

Principal Stewart scratched his chin before giving a curt nod. Lilith's fingertips were so cold she could barely feel them as she finished clasping the purifier around her neck again. She hesitated before letting go of the string—but she'd taken Life Powder from two strangers, teleported, and even translated a language she had never studied. She had to be able to do something on purpose for a change.

C'mon. Lilith pulled her focus together and fixed her gaze on the blue circle, feeling a tingling warmth in her fingers and toes. This time, she traced her bare wrist. The air hummed and—*whoosh!* Blue sparkles formed around her. In the blink of an eye, she was standing on the blue circle.

Relief flooded her veins. But there was no applause. No cheers. Principal Stewart simply snapped his fingers, resetting the hourglass and revealing new instructions for the next task: to teleport back to the white circle, then next to a black box filled with Life Powder. Lilith cracked her knuckles and stared at the first circle—*whoosh.* It was like ticking a checkbox inside her head.

Thick smoke erupted from the ground before she could teleport again. *Not fair.* Lilith thought, trying to see the black box behind the swirling haze—impossible. Still, she straightened her back, wiggled her fingers and tried her best.

Her first attempt landed her in the bleachers. The second sent her into the hallway between the arena and the entrance. And, by the third, she somehow ended up on the teachers' platform—face-to-face with Principal Stewart. Lilith's heart leaped to her throat. At least fifteen apologies tumbled out of her mouth in under a minute.

Each failure chipped away at her confidence. Thirteen tries. Thirteen wrong turns. The arena spun around her, nausea hitting her hard. Lilith braced her hands against her knees, breath ragged, just as the last grain of sand slipped through the hourglass. The teachers exchanged uneasy looks, all turning to Principal Stewart, as if they expected him to say something.

"Professor Thomas," Principal Stewart finally called, his voice breaking the tension. "Miss Fletcher could use one of your restorative teas."

The teacher in the red suit nodded and carried a cup down from the platform without spilling a drop. "Hello, dear," she said in a warm, regal tone. Her deep-brown complexion glowed under the soft light. Meticulously groomed brows and long lashes framed her keen eyes, and delicate black braids wove into a fishtail that brushed her waist. "Have this before the next task. It'll help you feel better." She smiled, extending the cup. "I'm Professor Thomas."

"Thank you," Lilith said softly, sniffing the tea. "Ginseng, orange... something else?" she wondered. The brew smelled heavenly and Lilith didn't hesitate to gulp it down. Relief spread through her like a drought-stricken flower soaking up water.

"You know your herbs," Professor Thomas observed, eyes gleaming. "It's a special brew, made with my own secret spell. Loopers usually aren't that familiar with nature's properties—you must have a knack for it. Where'd you learn about tea?"

"I just... always kind of liked it, I guess," Lilith said, checking the empty cup and wishing for more.

"I hope you'll stop by the greenhouse, even though Loopers don't need botany-related classes—or maybe you could use an extracurricular? Oh, and here's your very first skill badge for Teleportation." She handed Lilith a bronze pin while retrieving the empty mug.

On the panel below the platform, the first slot beneath the Looper's symbol now displayed a bronze figure: solid head and shoulders, its lower half striped and fading away. Lilith carefully fastened it below the Looper's crystal badge.

"I have to get back up there, but you're doing great, dear," Professor Thomas added before returning to the platform. The warmth of her kindness lingered, but so did the pressure in Lilith's chest. The assessment wasn't over yet, and she had no idea if she was ready for whatever came next.

CHAPTER EIGHT

THE UNEXPECTED

Anticipation hung in the air as Lilith stood at the center of the expansive arena. Her shoulders tightened, but she had done it. She had teleported on her own—and nobody had gotten hurt in the process. A flicker of determination sparked inside. "I'm ready," she said, voice steady.

Principal Stewart nodded and flicked his finger, making the hourglass flip again. Lilith drew a slow breath and blew it out as her eyes moved to the glowing instructions for the next task: move Life Powder from the black box to the white one. The words echoed in her head. *Life Powder*. Just hearing it again made her stomach twist. But no humans were involved this time. She clung to that.

"All right, Lilith. You've got this," she whispered.

A surge of energy tingled in her hands. Lilith squared her stance, leaned forward, and leveled her gaze at the black box before cupping her palms into a dome. "Up. Up." Her lips moved, though no sound came out. The powder glittered, then lifted, rising in a delicate stream.

"It's floating!" Kallista squealed from the platform, her excitement mirroring Lilith's own.

But Lilith didn't glance at the platform—her focus stayed locked on the fragile, glowing dust, as if she were carrying a glass sculpture through a windstorm. Step by careful step, she guided it through the air and lowered it into the white box. The instant it touched down, the box turned black.

Done. Lilith exhaled hard, arms dropping, her muscles trembling with relief. But there was no break this time. New instructions appeared on the panel almost instantly: wither a flower. Her breath hitched. A jolt of dread coursed through her chest, dredging up dark memories. Her fingers curled against her palm. For one awful second, the flower wasn't a flower at all. It was the boy in the street. The man in the park. Life Powder lifting when she hadn't meant to take it.

She squeezed her eyes shut. *It's not a person,* she told herself, reopening her eyes. "Sorry, little flower," she whispered, voice tight. Stepping back, she trailed her fingertip along the infinity mark on her wrist. A shimmer pulsed through her fingers and the petals shriveled. The flower wilted as Life Powder drifted into the air like shimmering ash.

Lilith clenched her fist, drawing the powder inward. The task was done. *But was it? Something was missing.* The instructions said nothing about keeping the flower like that. Even as the hourglass flipped, her fingers slowly opened. Carefully, almost guiltily, she guided the powder back to the stem as new instructions appeared, like she was sneaking a stolen cookie back into the jar and hoping no one noticed. The plant stirred. Then it bloomed—softly, beautifully, fully. Warmth rushed through her like sunlight after rain. Giving Life Powder... it felt different.

She smiled, lifting her gaze to the panel. It was time to raise Life Powder from the box and shape it into an animal. *Shape it?* Lilith frowned, eyeing the container filled to the brim with Life Powder. She lifted a dusty, lopsided cloud into the air, slowly compacting it into a sphere.

Lilith concentrated on the shape of a bat: wings, ears, tiny claws. But instead of taking shape, the orb burst apart, scattering Life Powder like a miniature dust storm. A fine mist billowed upward, settling in her hair and—when she gasped—coating her tongue with a dry, gritty film. *Great. Now she'd eaten Life Powder, too.* Lilith clamped down on the thought before her mind could spiral any further.

"Sorry," she sputtered. Life Powder covered the arena. It looked like a fairy-dust bomb had exploded, sprinkling everyone from head to toe. At least now she was sure it wouldn't animate random objects like she'd considered—*and hopefully none of her organs, either.*

"That's quite all right, Miss Fletcher," said a short, round teacher with rosy cheeks. His mustache merged into a beard that obscured his neck, and his large button nose gave him a friendly look. He stood and waved his hands in a slow, rhythmic pattern. The powder gathered as though invisible brooms were sweeping it up. "There, there," the teacher murmured once the powder had settled back into the box.

"Much appreciated, Jonathan," Professor Thomas said, lightly brushing her shoulder free of powder.

"Of course, of course," the teacher replied, hopping toward Lilith. On the panel below the platform, the second slot lit up with a new symbol. "Your badge, missy," he said, tipping his Indiana Jones–style hat in greeting before handing her a silver pin. "I'm Professor Jonathan Goldsmith," he said, "and welcome to A.M.A."

"Thank you, Professor Goldsmith. Sorry again about the mess," Lilith said, picking at her thumbnail.

"No worries," he said, putting his hat back on. "Happens more often than you'd think." His eyes crinkled into a cheery grin as he clapped and rubbed his hands before shuffling back to his seat.

Lilith peered at her shiny new pin, its surface engraved with a small mound of grains—clearly representing Life Powder. *How many badges did one person need?* she wondered. She tried to fasten it beneath the others, but her fingers fumbled with the clasp. Once. Twice. By the time it finally clicked into place, her arm felt too heavy to lift.

Then the hourglass flipped again. She glanced toward Professor Thomas's teapot before she could stop herself. No such luck.

"Wait—Levitate?" Lilith's mouth fell open. *Seriously? She could fly?* Lilith shook her head, trying to wrap her mind around a skill she hadn't even realized she had. And the instructions weren't much help; the tiny figure on the panel simply floated there, as if that explained everything. She gave jumping a try, but gravity pulled her right back down. Then she stood on her tiptoes, arms stretched high, breath shaky. *I can float,* Lilith told herself. Eyes closed, she pushed against an invisible barrier, imagining a calm, buoyant motion. Her stomach swooped. The floor dropped away, and empty air rushed beneath her shoes.

Lilith's eyes shot open. The world tilted like a merry-go-round. Then she lost her balance and crashed down, arms flailing in a pointless effort to catch herself. "Ow!" she groaned. It had barely lasted a second or two, but... *had she just floated? For real?*

"Professor Homolka," Principal Stewart called. "Will you?"

Still on her knees, she looked up as a teacher with short, stark-white hair, seated two chairs from Principal Stewart, slowly raised her head. A chill crawled over Lilith's skin. Every breath caught in her throat. Professor Homolka was pale in a way that didn't look sick or old, but ancient, like the moon had drained all the warmth from her skin. One eye was a murky grayish-white, and crooked yellow teeth peeked between her thin lips.

A blue flash split the air. Professor Homolka vanished from the platform and reappeared directly in front of Lilith, close enough for Lilith to see every crease in her ancient-looking face.

"Your Levitation badge," she said tonelessly, her eerie eye fixed on Lilith's.

Lilith cleared her throat, unsure which eye to focus on, her heart hammering inside her chest. "T-thank you," she mumbled, taking the wooden pin shaped like a seated, meditating figure. She took an unnecessarily long time fastening it to her jacket, *which was definitely about precision and not about avoiding Professor*

Homolka's face. But by the time she finished, the professor was back in her seat.

Okay. One more task done, Lilith told herself, though she had no idea how many were left—or if she would still be able to survive them all. She exhaled, stood, and looked toward the panel. The next task was already there: travel back in time.

Wait. If time travel was real, she could go back and undo things. No more Academy. No more Life Powder. No more waking up in a world where nothing made sense. No more being afraid she would hurt strangers. *A way out.* A flutter of hope sparked in her chest.

She was supposed to go back as far as possible, find the red stone in the middle of the arena, and read the paper hidden beneath it. But Lilith wanted to go somewhere else—to her fourteenth birthday, to the moment she decided to go to the bakery. She took a deep breath and closed her eyes. *I have to go back. I can fix this. Back, back, back.* She wished until every part of her seemed to pull toward the past.

But instead of hearing Amy giggling during bath time, Lilith heard herself saying "sorry" and frowned. There it was: another version of herself, covered in golden dust, with Professor Goldsmith coming to her rescue during the Life Powder shaping task. She had gone back in time—but no more than ten or fifteen minutes.

The colors around her looked wrong, as though the world had dissolved into muted hues. Lilith frowned. She had to try again.

But it didn't matter how much effort she poured into it. Each attempt drained more of her energy and only let her slip back a few extra seconds. Frustration gnawed at her as she slowly shook her head, letting defeat settle in. If she couldn't fix the past, the least she could do was finish the task. Lilith scanned the arena, spotted the rock, grabbed the paper, read the message, and sank to the ground. Not to catch her breath, exactly. Mostly because she had no idea how to get back to the present. Her muscles ached. Her mind felt foggy. So she waited for time to catch up. She was more exhausted by the second.

Green and violet light eventually erupted around her, and the paper between her fingers dissolved into thin air. She was no longer sitting. Now Lilith was standing exactly where she had been before traveling back. She blinked.

"Miss Fletcher?" Principal Stewart prompted from the platform. The hourglass next to him was now empty.

"Huh? Yes. Uh, I—" She shook off the daze. "Caught between Scylla and Charybdis," she recited, recalling the phrase from the paper.

Principal Stewart nodded to the teachers before descending from the platform himself. Lilith swallowed. Somehow, that felt more official than the other teachers coming down. He handed her a wooden badge and told her that the paper beneath the rock had been enchanted to change as time passed. The pin featured an intricately engraved clock, its delicate arrows and gears interwoven like a secret waiting to be unraveled. Lilith murmured a thanks as she fastened it onto her jacket, still trying to wrap her mind around the fact that time travel was apparently real.

The hourglass flipped again, and Lilith scrubbed at her eyes, her mind sluggish from the relentless tasks. But this had to be the last one. Only one badge slot remained empty on the panel. She swallowed hard and read the instructions. Converse with a

Litticon. Just talk. Her shoulders dropped for the first time in what felt like forever.

The creature perched on a rock was tiny and rail-thin, with wide, knowing eyes fixed on her. Lilith pushed through the fatigue, cycling through forty-two different languages. Words flowed almost instinctively, her brain barely processing each switch. As the final syllable left her lips, the hourglass on the platform gave a soft clink, its remaining grains vanishing into nothing. A golden *Hyperpolyglotism* badge shimmered into existence, filling the last empty slot on the panel. A deep, unsteady breath escaped her.

Lilith would've jumped around if she weren't so wiped out—or maybe floated around if she'd mastered levitation. Instead, she let herself quietly revel in victory. She had done it. No one harmed. Her muscles ached as tension drained from her shoulders. Maybe, just maybe, the Academy wasn't as scary as it had seemed. She could be okay here while she figured out what came next.

"Miss Fletcher?" Principal Stewart called, his expression serious.

Lilith stiffened, her pulse racing. *What now?* She hadn't cheated or anything. *Why was everyone staring at her?*

"Look behind you!" Kallista hollered, leaping from her seat.

CHAPTER NINE

CHRYSANTHEMUM'S MYSTERY

At first, Lilith braced herself for a troll or even a dragon looming behind her. She summoned every ounce of courage to turn around. But instead of some monstrous beast, she found something entirely unexpected—a trail of bright yellow flowers blooming in the dirt where she had just stepped.

Lilith tilted her head. *Why was everyone so astonished?* She had already teleported, levitated, spoken in forty-two languages, and traveled back in time. She had even collected Life Powder from two people before knowing she had powers. Yet somehow, producing flowers had caused the biggest stir of all.

She knelt and brushed her fingers over the petals—nothing special.

"You can evoke chrysanthemums?" Professor Thomas asked, her voice hesitant.

"I guess?" Lilith lifted an eyebrow as she turned around to face the teachers. The panel below the platform glowed, showing a new crystal slot beside her Looper's emblem, but it was empty. Her eyes narrowed—*wasn't the assessment supposed to be over?* She waited a beat, but the panel didn't add a new task this time. "Am I supposed to be doing something?"

"Well, instructions can only be tailored once we know which deity gifted you. Maybe try using your nature skill a bit more," Professor Thomas replied with a warm smile. "Maybe grow something again?" she added.

Which deity? Didn't her gift come from the Fates? Too many questions crowded her mind at once, tangling before she could say any of them out loud. Her gaze landed back on the yellow flowers. "More flowers," she said, raising her hand and wiggling her fingers experimentally. *Grow, grow,* she urged. But with questions tangling in her mind and every gaze pinned on her, concentrating was basically impossible.

Lilith closed her eyes and reached for the quiet thrum of life beneath her feet, picturing seeds cracking open, stretching toward the sun, golden flowers dancing in the breeze, and apple trees heavy with fruit. *Come on,* she urged. But not even a thorn or a leaf appeared.

"I'm sorry," Lilith said. She glanced at the purifier around her wrist, deflated. "I don't know how."

"Mmm," Principal Stewart murmured, breaking the silence. "Tell me, Miss Fletcher... are you capable of anything else? Anything out of the ordinary?"

Out of the ordinary? He had to be joking. Everything at this place was out of the ordinary. What even counted as normal? Lilith shrugged. "I have no idea."

"Miss Fletcher seems exhausted," Professor Thomas interjected, her long braid shifting over her shoulder. "We can let her abilities develop through the year and assign new classes as her skills flourish. I've already reserved her spot in Nature Manipulation." She winked.

"Donna's right," Professor Lewis agreed. "A wood-level nature skill, plus an unknown badge, should suffice for now," he suggested.

"Fair," Principal Stewart said with a nod. "Welcome to A.M.A., Miss Fletcher." With a flick of his index finger, three badges shimmered into view and floated toward her.

Lilith caught them midair. One was gold, awarded for her fluency in so many languages. The second was wooden, with a delicate leaf carved into its center. The third was crystal—clear, cold, and etched with a single question mark.

"What does that mean?" Lilith asked, staring at the crystal one.

"That's a temporary unknown badge," Professor Lewis explained. "You've been gifted with more than we expected, but it is unclear where this additional gift came from. So we'll figure out which other deity marked you as your skills evolve."

"Another god? How can you tell?" Lilith asked, stepping closer to the platform.

"Loopers can't manipulate nature," he told her. "Since you grew flowers, it seems that when you accepted the Fates' gift, another gift awakened, too." His lips thinned. "But you're drained, classes start tomorrow, and you need rest. Let's not rush it."

"Indeed," Principal Stewart said. "Dormant skills will surface over time. Now, Miss Lambros," he turned to Kallista, "please show Miss Fletcher out and ensure her sunrise is synced for tomorrow. You're both excused."

"Yes, sir," Kallista answered, bounding down the steps like a gazelle. She grabbed Lilith's hand, giggling.

"Okay. T-thank you," Lilith yelped while Kallista pulled her away with surprising strength.

"That was so cool!" Kallista squealed as they walked down the small corridor, heading back to the dorm. "I also got a gold badge in my first assessment, but—you're a *hybrid*? That's amazing!" She grinned. "I've only met a few hybrids in my life."

"Hybrid?" Lilith echoed, raising her eyebrows.

"Yeah—someone gifted by more than one god," Kallista explained. "In your case, the Fates plus whoever's behind your nature skill. A friend's distant cousin was actually gifted by three deities at once—but he's a show-off," she said, wrinkling her nose.

"Couldn't we just check which god grants nature powers to figure it out?" Lilith asked matter-of-factly.

Kallista snorted. "There are hundreds of gods, goddesses, and beings who can do that. Don't worry, though. As you discover more hidden skills, you'll narrow it down by combining them and connect your abilities to the right deity."

"Okay—um, Kallista?" Lilith called, eyes widening as they stepped inside the Pi common area.

"Yeah?" Kallista replied, leaning in.

"Is that... a headless person?" Lilith asked, stopping short.

A figure with no head stood in front of the Theta room, its face set into its chest. Lilith's eyes narrowed... *What in the world? Was it carrying her suitcases and her backpack? That couldn't be right.*

"Shh!" Kallista hissed, pulling Lilith aside. "That's one of the Acephali. They keep this whole place running—they cook, clean, take care of everything. They're cursed creatures... and trust me, they're very vindictive. I heard a rumor about a third-year who kicked one as a 'joke.' And the Acephali got back at her by spitting in her food, smashing her packages, and even hiding poison ivy in her pillowcase! Not a day went by that she wasn't tormented by the Acephali until the day she left."

"It seems to me like that third-year deserved it." Lilith crossed her arms.

"I like how you think," Kallista said with a smirk. "Come, let's get you settled. And—be polite." With calm confidence, she approached the Acephali. "Hello. This is Lilith Fletcher. She's assigned to this room." Then she gently guided Lilith's wrist toward the doorknob.

Click. The door unlocked and the three of them stepped inside the room. The bed on the left side was still pristine—no books on the desk, no wrinkles in the sheets. Maybe Lilith didn't have a roommate at all.

"Please set her things by the desk," Kallista added.

"Sure, lazy lady," the Acephali grumbled, dumping everything where Kallista had pointed. "Humans never thank Norm," it huffed, stomping away.

"Oh—thank you, Norm!" Lilith called out.

Norm paused, eyes narrowed, before disappearing behind the door.

"Norm?" Kallista raised an eyebrow.

"Isn't that his name?" Lilith said with a shrug.

"Beats me. We have tons of Acephali," Kallista said, stretching her neck for a better look, but the creature was already gone. Then she checked her pocket watch. "Oh no—I'm going to be late for class. See you, Lilith!"

"See you," Lilith shouted back as Kallista dashed away in a blur.

The door closed with a soft click as she slipped off her jacket. Looking down at her pinned badges, she felt a quiet rush of pride mixed with fear. *A hybrid?* Lilith had always thought of herself as plain as a loaf of bread—*why would another deity choose her alongside the Fates?*

Frowning, she unpinned the question-mark badge and the leaf badge, turning them over in her hands. As if studying every inch of them would give her any answers. The crystal caught the light first, flashing cold and clear. Then the leaf badge gleamed against her palm. Lilith's breath slowed. *Unknown. Nature. Looper. Life Powder.* The words lined up in her mind like stepping-stones, though the last ones still made her stomach tighten.

What if everyone was wrong? What if being a Looper wasn't the only thing waiting for her at the Academy? What if this second gift meant she could do something other than collect Life Powder? Her fingers tightened around the two badges, holding on to hope. The magic world without the Looper part... that she could get used to.

Her phone buzzed, jolting her. She hadn't even realized it was among the things Norm brought over. Shaking her head, she set down the pins on her desk and rummaged through her backpack—somehow squeaky clean, with no trace of rain, dirt, or damage. *This world's magic, or Meghan's doing?* she wondered for a split second.

"Lilly!" Amy's squeaky voice burst through the phone. "I miss you! Are you at school? How is it? See anyone famous yet?" she babbled until Meghan's face appeared behind her.

"Hi, sweetie," Meghan signed with one hand as Amy bounced like popcorn, trying to get a better view.

"Hey, bud, we wanted to see how your new school is going. We miss you," Nicholas said, but only his forehead was in the frame.

It's going great, Lilith joked to herself. *I only killed two people this week, took a bizarre test, and unlocked superpowers.* Lilith forced a smile. "It's good," she replied. Her own voice sounded too smooth, too easy. *Shouldn't lying to her family be harder than this? But then again, wasn't her life already built on half-truths?* She lied every time she pretended she was fine. Every time she faked having friends. Every time she swallowed the truth: she wished Nicholas would stop burying her mother's memory deeper and deeper.

Even Nicholas lied. He said he didn't blame her for her mother's death, but how could he not? Her first breath had stolen the last of the woman he loved—not that Lilith blamed him for that. *No wonder lying came so easily now.*

They chatted for maybe thirty minutes before hanging up. Lilith exhaled, relieved. How could this strange place, where nothing made sense, feel more comfortable than home?

Her arm brushed the map, knocking it loose from its pocket. Lilith picked it up and stepped onto the small balcony next to her desk. She leaned against the railing and drew in a deep breath of fresh air. The clouds stretched endlessly in every direction. The fact that they were drifting around the globe was still settling in. Where were they now? Had the Academy already drifted somewhere else entirely—Australia, Brazil, maybe even somewhere near Illinois?

Lilith frowned as water spread over the tanned paper in her hand, sketching new details. "Huh?" Classes were supposed to start tomorrow. *Why was the map creating paths?* She ran her fingers over the worn edges and opened it curiously.

"Phaunos Tree," she read aloud. The words barely left her lips before realization slammed into her. "Oh, crumbs!" Lilith gasped, smacking a hand to her forehead as the Oracle's prophecy resurfaced. She was supposed to be there in eight minutes.

Eight minutes.

Her stomach flipped. *How was she supposed to pull that off?*

CHAPTER TEN

TICK-TOCK

What would it mean not to fulfill an Oracle's prophecy? Lilith shivered at the thought as she raced out of the Zeus Wing, hoping she wouldn't have to find out. She glanced at her map, trying to follow its directions, hurrying through the Diplomatic Terrace. She rounded the next corner too fast, eyes glued to the map, and walked straight into something very solid and very much alive. One second she was running. The next, she was on the floor.

"Ow!" she exclaimed, rubbing her forehead. "I'm so, so, so sorry," she added without lifting her gaze from the parchment. "Ugh," she groaned. "There's no way I'll make it in time."

"You really like the floor, don't you, Feisty?" a familiar voice said. Lilith looked up. *Adrien? Of all people?*

"Sure, I love the view from down here," she replied, sarcasm dripping from every word.

"Where are you rushing off to?" Adrien asked, craning his neck toward her map as she pushed herself up.

"Curious much?" Lilith shot back. "Well," she sighed, puffing out her cheeks, "I'm supposed to be at the Phaunos Tree by 3:09, but there's no way I'll make it. It's way too far." Her lip curled slightly in a near-pout.

"That time is... oddly specific," Adrien said, glancing at the watch strapped to his right wrist. "We're cutting it close, but I know a shortcut." He beckoned with a grin. "Follow me."

"Um, sure," Lilith muttered. She had to at least try.

Adrien zipped through two short corridors. Lilith's lungs screamed in protest, but he kept running as lightly as a feather. He was fast—bicycle-fast. "Need... air..." Lilith gasped, stopping and bending over. Her thighs burned. Maybe she should've taken P.E. more seriously.

"No breaks," Adrien announced, tugging her sleeve.

"You're enjoying this, aren't you?" Lilith panted. Adrien's rosy-cheeked grin confirmed her suspicion. How did he not have a single bead of sweat?

"Hi, Adrien!" three girls called in unison as they passed.

He shot them a wink, then turned back to Lilith. "So, how was it with Professor Lewis? Are you ready to become an actual Looper now?"

"It was... intense. And no, I'm definitely not ready to be a Looper," she said between breaths. "But I do have—" she paused for effect, "—a plan."

"A plan?" Adrien asked, jogging backward.

Showing off much? A fake pout tugged at her lips as she rolled her eyes. "Yeah. I'm gonna talk to the Fates and return my gift," she said between ragged breaths.

"So you just happen to have the siren's feather and all the stuff you need for the ritual lying around?" Adrien teased.

"What?" Lilith frowned, nearly doubling over from exhaustion.

Adrien chuckled. "Oh, Feisty! You can't just talk to a deity whenever you want. There are rituals, ingredients, offerings..."

"Whatever... I'll figure it out. How hard can it be to grab some ingredients?" she said, even as her legs started questioning every life choice that had brought her there.

"Really? You're such a rookie! You'd better come up with a backup plan. Now, come on—we're almost there." He waved her forward, and she groaned, thankful that despite being wobbly, her legs were still moving.

"Did you just call me Feisty and rookie in less than ten seconds?" She scoffed. "From what I've heard, I collected someone's Life Powder the same day I got my purifier... while it took you, what—a week to move one grain, Mr. Know-It-All?"

"Touché." Adrien smirked, then glanced around, slowing to a stop as they stepped into a narrow hallway. His eyes darted down both ends, like a kid about to cause trouble, before he started patting the wall. "Come on, help me find the knob," he whispered.

Stone walls didn't exactly scream giant tree, but Lilith was too busy being grateful for the break to argue. One more minute of running and her lungs, her legs, or both would've given up. Then Lilith checked the walls. No tree paintings. No sculptures. She arched an eyebrow. *That had to be a joke. Were people watching to see if she'd fall for it?* Before Lilith could decide whether this was a prank, Adrien jerked his chin toward the wall.

"Got it!" He hunched his shoulders, glanced up and down the hall, and grinned. "Come on," he said, twisting something invisible on the wall. With a soft scrape, a hidden section of cement swung open, revealing a doorway. Lilith's mouth formed a small "o," heat prickling at her cheeks. "Let's go. Move," Adrien called over his shoulder as he stepped through.

Lilith shook off her hesitation and followed. "Is that the Phaunos Tree?" she asked, peering down the steep slope beyond.

"Yep," Adrien said, shutting the hidden door behind them.

"For the love of waffles!" Lilith blurted. "We've got, like, three minutes! How are we supposed to get all the way down there in time?"

"Like this." Adrien touched the purifier around his wrist, and in seconds, a swirl of Life Powder spun into a shimmering disk before him.

"Uh…" Lilith tilted her head as the dust thickened and curved into a wide, bowl-shaped sled under Adrien's feet.

"You coming or what?" he asked.

"All right, all right," Lilith replied, stepping onto the wonky, rubbery platform. She sank slightly, struggling to stand upright.

"Hold on!" Adrien yelled.

"There's nothing to hold on to, genius!" she snapped, grabbing for the rim of the disk just as it lurched forward, hurtling down the slope at a terrifying speed.

More than halfway down, they hit a bump, and the sled launched into the air. Lilith's stomach flipped as they soared before crashing back down with bone-rattling force. The impact sent them tumbling, a chaotic blur of flailing arms and legs. Adrien lost control of the powder, and the disk shattered apart, dissolving all around them. Lilith rolled downhill, unable to stop herself, until she smacked into the dirt.

Her vision blurred as she struggled to find her bearings. Then—*pressure*. A heavy weight pinned her down. A groan escaped her lips as realization hit. Adrien had landed on top of her. "Get off!" she hissed, squirming beneath him and shoving him aside.

"Sorry," Adrien said, rolling onto his knees and collecting the scattered powder back into his purifier. "But hey—we made it," he added.

Lilith blinked, adrenaline surging. "We did it. We actually did it!"

"You guys okay?" asked a short, round-cheeked boy, maybe two inches shorter than Lilith. "That was so awesome! Are you two my teammates?" He grinned, showing the gap between his front teeth.

"Sorry, man, I'm already on a team," Adrien replied, cracking his neck and wincing at a scratch on his forehead. "I'm Adrien, by the way, and this is Lilith."

"Oh, too bad. I'm Jake," the boy said, his hazel eyes shining behind a pair of rectangular frames. "Here, I think you need this more than me," he added, pulling out a small tube from his pocket and handing it to Adrien. "Made it in my healing class last week."

"You're a lifesaver. Thanks," Adrien said, squeezing out a mustard-colored paste. He spread it over his palms and forehead, then extended the tube to Lilith. "Go on," he said impatiently. The paste absorbed into his skin, and in seconds, his wounds were gone.

"W-what—" she stammered.

"Just do it, Feisty!" Adrien urged, tapping his watch.

"Okay, okay," Lilith grumbled, crouching to dab the ointment onto her scraped knee. "Ugh, my tights are already ruined," she muttered. The salve stung for a split second—then, the raw scrape faded, skin knitting together as if nothing had ever happened. Lilith's eyes widened.

"I know we can regenerate pretty quickly, but it never hurts to speed it up," Adrien joked, winking at Jake.

Regenerate? Lilith tried to absorb his words. *It was like she was a superhero—except instead of saving people, she killed them.*

"Oh, hey! It's 3:08. Mission accomplished," Adrien said, puffing out his chest. "Good luck, Feisty." He shot her a playful salute.

"Thanks, Adrien," she replied. He bowed, then jogged off.

She had made it in the nick of time. *But now what?*

CHAPTER ELEVEN

A DIRTBAG MAKES THREE

As Adrien walked away, a crisp breeze rustled the massive tree's branches, sending a shower of golden leaves spiraling through the air. Lilith inhaled deeply, savoring the coolness. Autumn had always been her favorite season, and this spot could have been the definition of fall, even if, technically, it was spring back home.

One leaf drifted past, catching the last glimmers of sunlight before settling at her feet. *The ones she needed. What had the Oracle meant by that?* Lilith checked the time on her phone. It was now 3:09.

Heat flared across Lilith's wrist. She gasped and stumbled back. *No, no, no. Not again.* Professor Lewis had said she wouldn't have to collect Life Powder as long as she was on Academy grounds. *So why was her wrist acting up?*

The golden glow pulsed, curling up her arm like it had a mind of its own. "Jake, run!" she choked out. "I don't know how to stop it—it'll steal your Life Powder!" Panic cut through her, sharp and electric.

Jake's eyes flicked to her wrist. But instead of bolting, his shoulders eased. "It's okay," he said with a small, knowing smile. "It's gold."

Lilith hesitated, heart still hammering. "I—why is it glowing?" she muttered, flexing her fingers as if that would make it stop.

Jake grinned. "Because it's time to connect." He shoved up his sleeve, revealing a lyre-shaped mark—the same golden hue as hers. "I can't believe it," he mumbled, half to himself.

"You've got to be kidding me," a gruff, unimpressed voice cut through the air. Lilith squinted against the sunlight.

A boy sat at the base of the tree's trunk, arms crossed, pure irritation written across his face. *Had he been there the whole time?*

He let out a slow, exasperated sigh. "First-years. Really?"

"Connect? So, are you two the ones the Oracle meant?" Lilith raised an eyebrow and followed Jake toward the other boy.

"Oracles," the boy at the tree's base huffed. "Father is going to kill them for this." A lightning-shaped mark glowed on his pale skin, contrasting starkly with his onyx hair and emerald-green eyes. "Who are you?" he asked, eyes landing on Lilith.

"Lilith Fletcher," she answered, trying to sound composed. "You?" The boy turned to Jake.

"I'm Jake. Jake Sullivan Hills," he managed, fiddling with his sleeve.

"I am Arthur Owens, second-year, gifted by Zeus," the boy said, standing.

"Owens?   Like Jonathan-Owens-the-one-who-saved-the-school   Owens?" Jake blurted, eyes shining.

Arthur pressed his lips tight, making the scar near the corner of his mouth more pronounced. "Yes. That would be my great-great-great-grandfather," he said flatly.

"Oh, my Olympians! I'm teamed up with an Owens?!" Jake nearly squeaked, and Arthur rolled his eyes in response. "This is the best day of my life!" he continued, practically hugging his glowing lyre mark.

A warm golden string rose from Lilith's wrist, swirling upward to meet matching threads from Jake and Arthur. The three strands merged into one glowing line that turned white—then each thread returned to them, vanishing beneath their skin.

"Whoa," Jake murmured.

"What just happened?" Lilith asked, somewhere between mesmerized and confused.

"We just became a team," Jake said, grinning ear to ear. "Bonded for life!"

Lilith's heart lurched. "For *life*?" Panic crept into her voice. "I mean, I'm trying to give my gift back to the Fates," she admitted, chewing her lip. "I'm not actually staying here."

"So you're saying this is a temporary arrangement," Arthur chimed in, stepping forward. "That would make more sense. If you quit being a Looper, we'll get reassigned." He shrugged. "Maybe Father won't need to kill the Oracles after all," he added, his voice so dry it was hard to tell if he was joking.

"Teams 101, here we come!" Jake said, bouncing like a kid on Christmas morning.

"Great," Arthur muttered. "Another useless class with two first-years as my teammates."

"Rude much?" Lilith snapped, squaring her shoulders. Just because Arthur stood half a head taller didn't mean she had to shrink. "Who do you think you are, talking to people like that?" Her eyes narrowed. Nothing irritated her more than people who acted like they were above everyone else.

Jake sidled away, suddenly fascinated by the tree bark. Arthur's brows knitted; he touched the scar near the right side of his mouth. "Mmm," he said, his tone shifting. "I apologize for my rudeness."

Lilith narrowed her eyes, still suspicious. Was that an actual apology or sarcasm?

Arthur cleared his throat. "Anyway, I'll see you both around. If not, next week in class." With a curt nod, he turned on his heel and strode toward the Academy buildings—like nothing had happened.

Lilith scoffed, watching him go. "Seriously? What a dirtbag. Talk about mood swings."

"That was... amazing," Jake gushed, turning to Lilith. "Seriously. I wanna be just like you when I grow up! I mean—you know what I mean."

She snorted, then glanced at Arthur's retreating figure in the distance. "What's up with him? Was that some kind of joke? Because I didn't get it."

Jake shook his head. "Nah, he was actually sorry," he said, lowering his voice. "Guilty, even."

Lilith frowned. "Guilty? What do you mean?"

Jake rubbed the wooden pin on his jacket, hesitating. "Empathy skill. I'm still figuring it out—my dad says I should keep the blocker off to practice. But yeah, Arthur's not bad. I'd say he's even... scared? Wait. Please never tell him I said that."

Lilith pressed her lips together, biting back a laugh. *Jake was worried about Arthur finding out he was defending him? That was gold.* She gave him a small nod, shaking off the thought before refocusing. "Hmm. So what's the deal with his great-great-whatever grandfather? You made it sound like a superhero."

"Oh!" Jake's eyes lit up. "But it's true! Jonathan Owens saved all the academies from a big rogue attack, forever ago."

"Okay, seriously—someone *has* to define 'rogues' for me. I keep hearing about them and still have no idea what they actually are."

"Rogues are corrupted apprentices," Jake explained, grimacing. "They run around stealing Life Powder, controlling people, and building their power. They're hard to catch. And if they do get caught, their memories vanish—no one can recover them, not even top Mnemosyne experts. The Council can sentence them to have their marks disabled and send them home to live human lives, with no memory or gifts."

Lilith's eyes lit up. "Wait—you can remove someone's gift and send them home?"

Thank you, Oracle, for leading me here! Hope surged in her chest, bright and sudden.

Jake waved his arms frantically. "Not like that! That's a punishment for rogues, not an escape plan. If someone forcefully deactivates a mark outside a sentence from the Council, it's considered a betrayal to the gods. That means your soul gets tainted, and—" He took a breath. "You end up in Tartarus. Trust me, you do NOT want that."

Lilith pulled a face. "So Tartarus is some torture pit?"

Jake nodded. "Where souls get punished for their wrongdoing."

She scowled, flopping onto her back with a sigh. "Ugh. Fine. Another roadblock. Anyway, you were saying?"

Jake brightened. "Yes! A long time ago rogues tampered with multiple academies' flight paths, almost causing them to crash. Jonathan Owens harnessed Zeus's wind powers. Then he coordinated the abilities of alumni around the world to shift all the schools back on course. He saved everyone, but he didn't survive." Jake's tone softened. "The globe in our dining hall is called the Owens Tracking System—OTS—after him."

"Oh! I've seen the globe! And—whoa, that's crazy," Lilith said, eyebrows raised. "Too bad his descendant didn't seem to inherit the charm." She rolled her eyes.

A loud growl escaped from Lilith's stomach, and both of them burst into laughter.

"I'm guessing you're ready for food. I know I am," Jake said, bouncing slightly on his heels. "We could head to the dining hall.

And I could, um, fill you in on the OTS and other cool stuff on the way. If you want, I mean."

"Yes, please!" Lilith said. "But no running—or my lungs will definitely quit on me after the marathon I ran to get here," she teased, following him toward the main building.

CHAPTER TWELVE

WILD EMPATHY

B y the time Lilith and Jake reached the dining hall, he had pointed out more artifacts than she could count, including a mirror that only reflected lies, a fountain that changed flavor depending on who drank from it, and a statue that sneezed whenever someone said "Zeus."

"I love this place," Lilith said between mouthfuls, taking in the buzzing energy of the dining hall—laughter, clinking plates, and the occasional flicker of magic midair.

Jake, however, had his gaze fixed above. "There it is," he said, nudging her. "The Owens Tracking System." He gestured toward the massive globe overhead—the one Kallista had shown Lilith earlier. Its surface flickered with tiny sparks orbiting like fireflies, each marking a different academy. He grinned, already launching into an excited explanation. "That one? That's us, hidden by storm clouds. That one over there? It's underground, inside a mountain. And that one?" His voice dropped to a conspiratorial whisper. "Looks like an ordinary island—but beneath it? A whole underwater city."

After devouring three dark-chocolate pancakes drenched in raspberry sauce, Lilith eyed the omelet near the cereal station but decided her stomach couldn't fit more food for the next twelve hours at least. She cleared her throat, craving a drink. Meghan had always insisted Lilith was too young for coffee... But if she was old enough to assist with death, then caffeine should be fair game, right?

"Ewwww!" Lilith spat the black liquid back into the mug, and Jake burst out laughing. *Meghan was right yet again.* Lilith rolled her eyes. "Jake? How do you know so much about everything?" she asked, reaching for a glass of milk this time. Jake blushed.

"I don't know everything, not even close. But my family's been gifted by Apollo for generations, so I grew up around all this," he said, setting down his fork.

"I thought marks only got activated at fourteen?" Lilith narrowed her eyes.

Jake shrugged. "They do. But children from gifted parents can borrow magic to practice until they turn fourteen. My folks used to transfer energy to me so I could cast small spells, even as a toddler."

"So, kids from gifted parents don't really get a choice? You kinda have to accept your gift either way?" Lilith frowned at how unfair that sounded.

"What? No, we have a choice!" Jake said quickly. "But if I refused my gift, I'd lose my memories. My parents would basically have to lie to me for the rest of our lives. We'd never really connect, you know? And I'd miss out on all of this. Nobody in their right mind would say no to magic and—" He stopped himself, cheeks reddening. "I mean... it's different for you," he added quickly. "You didn't grow up with this. Saying yes means being cut off from your family, and that probably feels as awful to you as saying no would feel to me."

Lilith waved a hand. "The problem isn't the magic—that part I can totally get used to," she admitted. "But I don't want to kill people for the rest of my life." Her voice wavered. "Why couldn't I have been more like you, or Kallista?"

Jake set down his glass, his expression growing more serious. Serious didn't quite fit him. "Lilith, right now I'm assigned to a Looper's team. It means I send souls to the underworld with you—I'm your Bridger. We basically share the same job description."

She blinked. "What do you mean? You don't collect Life Powder," she said, stacking her dirty dishes.

Jake followed her to the dish conveyor, pausing as if he were choosing his words. "Well, I collect souls. I say that counts." He shrugged. "Loopers manage Life Powder, but they don't do the job alone. Each Looper teams up with a Bridger, like me, who collects souls, and a Ranger, like Arthur, who keeps watch and protects the team. Together, we handle someone's passing. Not just you.

Apollo could've made me a healer or an oracle, but this team made me a soul collector."

Lilith frowned. If a Bridger could be gifted by Apollo, like Jake, or Hermes, like Hannah... could her role change at the Academy? "So if roles can change depending on the gift..."

"Not all gifts," Jake clarified. "Loopers will always be Loopers."

"Yeah, yeah. But what if a Looper was a hybrid..." Lilith asked, half to herself. "Could that change the whole 'collecting Life Powder' job?"

Jake blinked, staring at her. "Huh?"

Lilith exhaled sharply. "Okay, I found out I'm a hybrid at my assessment. I can grow yellow flowers or something—but no one knows which god gave me that gift. I even have a question-mark pin." She reached up instinctively to pat her chest, only to realize she had forgotten it in her room earlier. "Crispy crackers! I left the two other badges on my desk," she moaned, burying her face in her hands.

Jake, who had been watching her speak without moving a muscle, suddenly jolted upright. "You're...a hybrid?" His eyes widened, and then, as the realization hit him fully, he practically jumped in his seat. "You're a HYBRID?!"

"Yeah. And my question is: does that mean I could do something other than collect Life Powder? Maybe there's a different kind of three-person team, so we wouldn't have to be a Looper team at all?"

Jake was still reeling, hands twitching. "I'm teamed with an Owens *and* a hybrid?" He let out a short, incredulous laugh. "My parents are gonna freak out!" He puffed his chest out for a second, but cleared his throat when Lilith gave him *the* look. "Ahem, sorry. I got carried away. But to answer your question... the marks active on our wrists when the bond forms decide our roles. Yours had the Fates' symbol, so we were teamed up with you as a Looper. No way around it. Your extra abilities won't change your role, but they might help you do your job," he said. "Unless, you know, something happens and someone leaves the team. Then the deities reassign us."

"Ugh," Lilith muttered as they headed out of the dining hall. "That's not fair."

They both went quiet as the corridor leading to the Diplomatic Terrace swallowed their footsteps.

"There must be a way to talk to the Fates, right? Maybe if I can explain everything, they'll let me go. Adrien said something about ingredients?"

Jake's expression tightened. "Um. It's...not impossible, but it's tricky." He paused, rubbing the back of his neck. "There is a ritual," he admitted, though something in his voice sounded off. His eyes flicked toward the ground. "I can check my books. Make a list." His words came out slow, as if they were fighting their way out of his mouth.

"Something wrong? I don't want to make you uncomfortable. You don't have to talk to me about this."

"No, it's not that. I just—" Jake winced mid-word, cutting himself off. His body tensed, shoulders hunching.

"Jake? Hey, are you okay?" She grabbed his arm, feeling his muscles coil. "What's happening?"

He gritted his teeth. "I... I need my empathy blocker. There's this awful—ugh." His eyes snapped toward a partly open door to their left. He exhaled, then dragged Lilith toward it.

Inside, a voice—low and sharp as a knife—cut through the silence. "You're worthless."

Lilith's blood ran cold.

"A parasite who ruins everything," the voice continued, each word laced with venom.

Lilith didn't need fancy empathy to feel that wound. She stared at Jake. "That's what you felt?" He nodded, fists clenched.

"I apologize, Father," came a voice from inside.

Lilith didn't have to look to know who was speaking—*Arthur.*

"Did I say you could speak?" the man snapped.

Lilith turned toward the crack in the door. Electricity crackled around the man's fingers.

"Insolent," he said, flicking his hand. Arthur hit the floor, but he didn't fight back.

Lilith's heart hammered. The man stepped toward Arthur again, and she couldn't stand there and watch. "Good evening, Principal Stewart!" Lilith hollered, her voice echoing down the corridor.

Jake nearly choked. "Are you insane?" he mouthed, eyes wide.

"People like him only care if someone important is watching," she hissed under her breath before shoving Jake into a small recess in the wall, where they dropped onto a bench tucked inside.

"We are not done," Arthur's father barked as the door creaked open. He glanced down the hallway, as if checking for the principal. "Fix this."

His heavy footsteps reverberated down the corridor, then faded. Lilith's fingertips felt numb when new footsteps approached. She held her breath as Arthur walked past them, spine rigid and eyes fixed ahead. She started to stand, but Jake yanked her back down.

She glowered at him. "We need to check on him," she whispered urgently.

Jake shook his head. "Not now. Trust me," he said, voice trembling as he fumbled in his pocket, pulling out a leather band and wrapping it around his wrist. Exhaling, he leaned against the wall and closed his eyes.

Lilith just sat there until Jake finally reopened his eyes.

"Are you okay?" she asked softly, like each word needed padding. Jake nodded, still subdued. "Are you sure?" she pressed. He seemed like someone else compared to the excited, talkative Jake she had spent the last couple of hours with.

"Yeah. I'm good. We should go," he said, holding tight to the leather band as he stood. "See you tomorrow in Nature Manipulation?"

"Yeah," Lilith agreed sluggishly. "You sure you'll be okay?"

He nodded again. "The blocker's on. I just need to decompress," he said. With that, he mustered a wobbly smile, and they headed off to their own rooms in different parts of the Zeus Wing.

CHAPTER THIRTEEN

FROM STRANGERS TO ALLIES

The memory of Arthur's father crackling with electricity haunted Lilith as she tried to sleep. Even after she dragged her exhausted mind to bed, his venomous words kept replaying until she finally drifted into an uneasy doze.

She woke to sunlight washing over her face. *Too bright.*

Lilith squeezed her eyes shut again as the light stabbed through her lids. She blinked once, twice, tears prickling at the corners, then forced one eye open at a time.

"Whoa," she breathed, her jaw slack. *Was that... a hole in the ceiling?*

The sunrise Kallista had mentioned... was it literally made of sunbeams? Her gaze trailed upward, tracing the golden light filtering through. Did that mean her ceiling was made of clouds drifting overhead? Her mouth parted in awe.

Even with last night's memories still clinging to her, this magical morning offered a rare kind of peace—a quiet, breathtaking distraction.

Lilith rolled over, grabbing her phone. "6:45 A.M.?" she groaned—that was too early, especially after the day she'd had. But she crawled out of bed anyway. Her mind was already racing, so falling back asleep was impossible.

After a quick shower, she checked her knees and palms. No scratches. It was bizarre; she examined them twice.

Once she was dressed, she paused. "The badges," she blurted, turning around. This time, she would not forget them. Lilith grabbed the two of them off her desk and pinned them back on her jacket.

Next came the dreaded tie. "Ugh," she complained, tugging at the fabric.

Her attempt at a knot looked so lopsided it could have been a bow gone wrong. "Whatever," she muttered, rolling her eyes and letting the ends dangle from her neck. For a second, she glowered at the tie, as if it might magically fix itself. No such luck. Well, at least this time she had one.

Shrugging, she reached for her map. Water had spread across the parchment, and she couldn't help the spark of excitement in her chest—magic was still magic, even if the rest of that gift was a mess. Lilith traced her finger across the wet words.

> *I am pleased to hear you've been assigned to a team. I'll see you soon!*
> — *Professor A. Lewis*

Was being on a team really a good thing, though? With a sigh, she scribbled a quick thank-you note with her waterbub. The words shimmered before getting sucked into the parchment. Then she checked the time—good thing she got out of bed earlier than she needed, because she took way longer than planned to get ready.

After one last check, she stepped out of the room. If she was going to face her very first magical class, she would rather do it with a full stomach—not that she was actually hungry. Her stomach remained knotted from the night before.

"Good morning," Lilith greeted an Acephali who mopped the floor. It wasn't Norm; this one had a deep scar running down its left arm. The creature paused, lifting its lip in a silent snarl. Lilith quickened her pace, resisting the urge to stare.

Lilith scanned the breakfast tables, trying to decide whether she needed something substantial or could survive on an apple.

"Hi," came a soft voice. Lilith spun around to find Jake.

"Oh—hi," she replied. "How are you feeling today?" Dark shadows under his eyes hinted he hadn't slept much.

"I'm okay," Jake replied, though his quiet tone suggested otherwise.

"You're still wearing your blocker," Lilith observed, pointing at his arm.

"Yeah, I guess I had enough training yesterday," Jake said, shrugging. "I've got something for you, actually." He handed her an armful of books. "I highlighted the parts you need."

"Did you stay up reading all night?" Lilith asked, dropping into an empty seat at the nearest table.

"Reading distracts me," he said.

There were so many highlights and sticky notes throughout the books, it reminded her of cramming for finals. Lilith picked up the top neon note and read it:

> *Missing ingredients: siren's feather, minotaur's hair, python's scale*

She looked at Jake, puzzled. "Is this all I need to contact the Fates?"

"Technically," he said with a nod. "I can hook you up with the red, white, and black candles—all the basics, even Midas Elixir. But the feather, hair, and scale? Those are trickier."

"Thank you," Lilith exclaimed, hugging him. Jake's cheeks turned redder than the apples next to them. "How do I find the missing ones?"

Jake scratched his head. "We could try the Academy's lake for a siren's feather?" he suggested, sounding unsure.

Lilith blinked. "We?" she echoed.

"If you want my help, that is." He trailed off.

"Of course I do!" Lilith said, eyes bright. "I thought you might be mad at me after last night—you seemed upset about, y'know, when I yelled... I don't want to get you into trouble."

Jake frowned, staring at his hands. Lilith worried he might take back his offer, and a tense silence stretched between them.

"I'm sorry," Jake said at last.

"Sorry?" Lilith's brows knitted. *What in the world was he sorry for?*

"Yesterday, it felt like I was drowning in all the emotions. It was too much." He rubbed the leather band on his wrist. "I wasn't mad at you for helping Arthur. To be honest, I was mad because I froze. But I was also relieved you were there." He looked up, his voice softer. "And I want to have your back the way you had his."

Lilith relaxed, warmth flooding her chest. "I'm lucky to have met you, Jake," she admitted. "And just so we're clear, I have your back too."

Jake's eyes sparkled. "Thanks, Lilith."

Just then, a familiar voice chirped, "Hello, hello, hello." Kallista bounded over, hands on her hips and grinning mischievously. "Shouldn't you two be heading to class already?"

Lilith and Jake laughed. After she grabbed an apple, they hurried off to her first-ever class at the Academy: Nature Manipulation. Unfortunately, the day's lesson was Herb Classification & Safety. Lilith had high hopes—*maybe they'd learn to mix healing ointments like the one Jake had used.* Instead, she spent an hour memorizing plant properties, toxicity levels, and which leaves could make someone woozy versus dead on the spot.

"Go on, take a sniff," Professor Thomas encouraged, handing out a sample.

Lilith leaned in, inhaling the scent of a sprig in her palm—only to gag at the rotten-egg-meets-sour-milk stench. "What is this?!" she choked out.

"Aconitum," the professor said with a bemused smile. "A powerful paralytic. Effective in small doses—lethal if mishandled."

Lilith pushed the plant as far away as possible while the students around scribbled notes. *Definitely not the kind of lesson she'd been hoping for.*

Still, nothing made her stomach twist more than stepping into Teleportation Intro class and spotting Arthur perched in the top row, his expression unreadable.

"Hi," Lilith greeted him awkwardly, sliding into the seat beside him.

Arthur offered a silent nod. *Was he mad? Annoyed? Did he even know they'd overheard him and his father?* Lilith's stomach flipped at the uncertainty.

"I thought you were advanced in teleportation?" she asked, trying to ease the tension after eyeing his badges.

"I'm the teaching assistant for this one," he answered.

Before she could respond, the professor clapped his hands. "Everyone, come, come." Students shuffled down the steps, gathering around the teacher's desk.

Arthur moved to follow, then suddenly muttered, "This professor is very particular about uniforms. You might want to fix that tie, Fletcher."

Lilith glanced down. "I... I've never worn one before," she admitted, standing up. "Actually, I've never even met anyone who wears a tie—not even my dad."

Arthur sighed, a quiet groan slipping past his lips. To her surprise, he stopped walking, turned around, and adjusted the tie for her with quick, precise movements. "There," he said, stepping back. His gaze flickered downward, lingering briefly. "Hybrid, huh?"

"Yep," Lilith confirmed. "Although all I know about my second gift is that I can grow flowers—maybe I'll start a cute garden?" she joked.

"Or a full forest," Arthur remarked.

Lilith opened her mouth, then closed it again. *Was that a compliment or something else entirely?*

Arthur added, almost offhandedly, "By the way, thank you for yesterday."

Lilith's eyes widened. *Was she imagining things? This definitely didn't seem like the same person she'd met by the Phaunos Tree.*

Arthur pivoted toward the stairs. "Move, Fletcher—everyone's already down there." Shaking her head, she hurried after him, determined to keep up.

By Friday, Lilith could teleport across a classroom without landing in a bookshelf, identify three poisonous herbs by smell, and say "I need a nap" in seven new languages. The Academy's classes were nothing like what she was used to—between trying not to explode Life Powder and keeping up with her language studies, she barely had time to process how much had changed. Still, she was learning. Even if her legs felt like jelly from dodging energy blasts and her brain threatened to melt from Hyperpolyglotism drills, she was getting the hang of things.

By the time they had their first Teams 101 class—an introduction to how gifted groups worked together—Lilith could already recognize a few faces in the crowd.

"Welcome, everyone!" Professor Lewis called from the front. "Today, we'll learn what it means to be part of a team. This is Teams 101, after all," he said with a warm smile. "My hope is that you'll learn from your mistakes and help all your classmates, even those who aren't on your team, throughout the semester."

Jake leaned over. "I'm so happy we didn't get Shivers for this class," he whispered. "The longer you avoid her, the better."

"Shivers?" Lilith raised an eyebrow.

"Professor Homolka. We call her Shivers because, well, you know," he explained with a shrug, and Lilith smiled wryly at the nickname.

Up front, Professor Lewis continued. "Being a team means you support each other. You must never leave all protection to the Ranger. Everyone is responsible for keeping the group safe and balanced. Today's special practice is simple: tag. You must tag out an opponent at least three times while avoiding being tagged yourselves. It ends when time's up or everyone on the team is tagged, whichever comes first."

Tag? There had to be a catch.

"No harmful skills," he added. "And no messing with other teams—just the one assigned against you." As he waved his hands, colored foam balls and matching bands appeared on each group's desk. "We'll head to the training grounds now. You'll find your assigned foes there."

Students rose in a flurry of chatter. Lilith, Jake, and Arthur exchanged glances. "Should we give all the foam balls to one person to control, or split them up?" Jake asked.

To her shock, both boys looked at her. *Shouldn't they be looking at Arthur?* "Um, split them, I guess? I'm no good at sports, so fewer for me, more for whoever's got better aim."

"Sounds good. Let's go," Arthur said, grabbing half the foam balls. Then Jake took a handful, and Lilith stuffed the rest into her pockets.

They headed to the training grounds while talking tag strategy. Jake's face lit up when they arrived at a wide-open field framed by trees, with throngs of students gathered. "I can't wait to see how it goes!" he said. Lilith smiled gently—this was the Jake she knew.

"Hills, take off your blocker," Arthur said.

Jake hesitated, touching the band. "Okay." He sighed and slid it off, positioning himself on his designated red spot.

Professor Lewis raised a dome-like shield overhead. Inside it, names, faces, and marks appeared for each student.

On the red team: a loop symbol for Lilith, lightning for Arthur, lyre for Jake.

"Luana's wing symbol means Hermes," Lilith noted, checking out their first opponent. "James is a Looper, and... what's the helmet on Cade's wrist?"

"Ares," Jake said grimly. "He's a Ranger. Ares grants weapon mastery, shapeshifting, time travel, weather, and energy blasts—they can do fireballs, too."

"Fireballs?" Lilith's mouth fell open. "How can we compete with that?"

"Hey." Arthur scowled. "You're our leader. Show some faith."

Me? Leader? Lilith tried to process it. *She usually ended up last-picked for any sports in P.E. She couldn't be their leader.*

"I have an advantage in weather, plus the Aegis shield to block projectiles. I also have telekinesis. And, like you, I can time travel—but better," Arthur said, shooting Lilith a look. "Plus, we've got shapeshifting if we need it. And Jake has his bow and good portal-manipulation skills. We'll excel—that's what I do."

"We got this," Jake agreed.

Lilith eyed them uncertainly. "Right," she said, forcing a nod. "Whoa." Lilith's mouth fell open as Professor Lewis sprouted olive trees, mud pits, and piles of sticks across the field, turning it into something like a magical paintball arena. Then snakes slithered in and owls swept down from every direction. "Yuck!" she yelped when a bright green serpent passed between her legs. "Why are there snakes?" She hated snakes.

"They're basically Professor Lewis's eyes—like referees." Jake suppressed a grin. "They won't hurt you."

Referees, sure, Lilith thought, shuddering. She gave her arms a quick shake, dispelling the clammy feeling.

"Everyone ready?" Professor Lewis called from the dome's edge, checking each group. "Tie your color bands so we can start." He stepped outside, clapping loudly, making a spark of light zip around the dome.

Then each team faced their assigned rivals. It was tag time.

Chapter Fourteen

A GAME OF STRATEGY

The training grounds fell silent as the dome overhead blinked twice, signaling the start of the match. Immediately, the students scattered like a bag of marbles spilled across the floor—each one disappearing behind trees, mounds, or even into thin air!

Lilith was still tying her red band when a wet splat echoed nearby. She ducked, checking her arms and legs before looking up. Yellow paint dripped down a transparent, blue-tinted shield in front of her. Luana had launched a projectile, but Arthur formed a shield—using his Aegis skill—to protect her.

Arthur hurled a red ball that clipped Luana's shoulder, forcing her to retreat. "Go, go, go!" he urged Lilith. Determination spread through her bones and she threw a red ball at Luana too—only to miss. Gritting her teeth, she sprinted for cover behind a nearby bush, and then edged toward a thicker tree trunk. Next time, she would be ready.

A girl suddenly popped up in front of Lilith, making her stumble back. The girl wore a purple waistband, though. *Not her opponent—good.* Then Lilith's eyes locked onto a yellow-banded boy crouched behind a pile of sticks—Cade. Somehow two red splotches already stained his uniform—one more and he'd be out. *I got this*, she told herself.

Lilith squared her stance and snatched a ball from her pocket like she actually knew what she was doing. It nailed Cade—eliminating him from the game. He cursed under his breath as the dome display flashed a red X over his picture. A rush of pride surged through Lilith—at least until a yellow ball splattered against the back of her neck. She spun around on the spot. Nobody could get tagged twice by the same opponent unless there was a thirty-second break between hits, which meant Lilith had maybe twenty seconds left to find the source before she could be tagged again. She frowned. *Where did that come from?* But there it was—fresh, muddy footprints. A grin spread across her face as she hurled a red ball above the trail, striking an invisible figure—Luana. The paint exploded across her, revealing her outline. Her face twisted in anger. Lilith let out a lopsided smile. Her old P.E. teacher would have been so proud.

Before Luana could throw another ball, Lilith dashed behind a stone, counting under her breath until she could target her opponent again.

"Eeeeeeek!" Lilith shrieked, nearly colliding with a snake. Heart pounding, she bolted toward another tree near the dome's edge.

"Jake, watch out!" Lilith yelped as a yellow ball shot toward him. But he didn't have nearly enough time to turn, let alone dodge. The ball struck him right in the chest. His last hit. He was out of the game too.

Jake sighed, swiping at the dripping paint. "It's fine. Go hide!" he called before trudging toward the sidelines, where the eliminated players sat outside the dome's boundaries.

Lilith groaned and pressed her back against a large rock. Above the field, another red X flashed across the dome projection, crossing out James's picture this time. *Arthur must have gotten him.* As far as their matchup went, only Luana mattered now.

"Excuse me," the rock barked.

"Whoa!" Lilith jumped back, her heart slamming against her ribs.

The boy lobbed a gray ball at someone, then shifted back into rock form. *People could turn into rocks too?* Lilith gaped. *Could they turn into trees? Bushes? Mud pits? Basically anything everyone else was using for cover?* That didn't sound particularly fair, but then again, neither did having an invisible opponent.

A noise behind her made her spin around, nearly beaning Arthur in the face with a red ball.

"Shhh!" Arthur hissed. "We've got less than twelve minutes before the game ends. We need a plan to tag Luana. Ideas?" He glanced over his shoulder. "Wait. We're too exposed. Meet me up there."

He jumped upward and vanished into the branches overhead. Lilith's eyebrows shot up. *Was there a springboard under his shoes?* She shook her head hard. *Was he aware she'd had exactly one teleportation class in her life?*

She grunted and tried anyway, looping a finger over her Fates' mark. Her toes tingled, and her eyes felt so dry she was afraid to blink. But it worked. She materialized on a thick branch, which would have been impressive if she hadn't immediately slipped on the rough bark. She flailed her arms like a useless chicken trying to fly, but Arthur caught her shoulder and steadied her.

"You really need some more basic training," he murmured, sounding half impressed, half exasperated. "Okay, any strategy?"

"Maybe one of us acts as bait and the other gets her?" Lilith suggested.

Arthur frowned as if she had insulted him. "No one gets sacrificed on my watch, Fletcher."

"Fine." Lilith glanced at the dome. Seven players remained in the dome, including them. "You know everyone's abilities, right? Do any of the other people have invisibility?"

Arthur studied the floating pictures above them. "We've got me, you, another Looper, an Artemis, a Demeter, a Poseidon, and Luana Marvis. No. None can turn invisible except her."

"Okay, then." Lilith nodded. "I think I've got an idea." She reached for Arthur's hand and set it on her shoulder. "Don't let go," she warned. Balance was definitely not her best skill.

Lilith traced the loop on her wrist, activating the Life Powder in her purifier, just like Adrien had done when he made that ridiculous sled to reach the Phaunos Tree earlier that week. But this time, she didn't need to hold a shape. She only needed to sweep it around.

The shimmering dust rose and rushed across the field. *Pffft!* It slammed into something invisible near the northern corner.

Arthur's eyes lit up. With his free hand, he pitched a red ball straight at the impact point, coating Luana in bright red paint. The dome flashed a final red X over her picture. Jake let out a triumphant yell from outside the dome, and Lilith couldn't help cheering too.

"Hey, are you smiling?" she teased.

Arthur looked away. Without replying, he tightened his grip on her shoulder and teleported them out of the tree, landing beside Jake on the sidelines. For the remaining minutes, they watched in silence as Professor Lewis had instructed.

"Time's up!" Professor Lewis proclaimed, dropping the dome with a resounding clap.

The professor systematically replayed each student's highlights and missteps on a glowing energy screen. Lilith's head spun with all the insights as he finally got to her.

"Why did Miss Fletcher get hit here?" he asked, showing a clip of Lilith's blunder.

"She didn't watch her back?" suggested a pointy-nosed boy.

Lilith winced—*that was true.* She'd barely realized the game had started altogether.

"Correct," Professor Lewis said. "How could she have avoided this?"

"A better hiding spot? Being faster?" a girl in red glasses ventured.

"Back-to-back with a teammate for full 360 coverage!" a purple-hatted boy shouted.

"She could've listened for footsteps or breathing," added a yellow-banded girl.

"All good answers!" Professor Lewis beamed. "We can all learn from these suggestions. Now, what was Miss Fletcher's greatest strength?"

"Powder manipulation," called a boy in the front row near Jake.

"She was persistent—she immediately fought back," another voice chimed in.

Professor Lewis nodded. "Great observations. Now, let's move on to Miss Marvis. How did she get hit?" He replayed each of Luana's hits.

"She misused her invisibility?" Jake said quietly.

"In a manner of speaking," Professor Lewis agreed. "Invisibility bends light, but it's draining; even a small lapse can make you visible, so it was a bold choice. Although Miss Marvis held her invisibility well, she forgot about her tangibility. How could she have fixed this?"

"Invisibility, by itself, is risky, but she could've stayed in a bush so the dust wouldn't outline her body as clearly, or circled back to her last cleared spot," Jake replied.

Gasps rippled through the students. Excited whispers filled the space; clearly, some were amazed by the new possibilities.

Professor Lewis smiled. "Great suggestions. Our abilities can be more complex than we think," he said before moving on.

Lilith found herself enthralled, not just because of the class or because she had actually helped her team win. She eyed Arthur.

He hadn't been tagged at all. Then she looked at Jake, who had managed to tag an Ares kid twice in the first five minutes using a bow with arrows made of pure energy.

There was so much to learn about everyone's gifts that by the time class ended, Lilith almost wished it could last longer. One thing was for sure: she needed to study more about deities, gifts, and skills before she had to face random opponents again.

CHAPTER FIFTEEN

BLENDER FALLS

As the final scoreboard flickered off, the dome overhead blinked twice. Professor Lewis snapped his fingers. Snakes slithered back into the grass, and owls took flight, their wings silent as they vanished into the sky. The terrain shifted seamlessly, blending the open field into the dense forest beyond.

Although students wandered toward the main building as soon as class was over, Lilith and Arthur lingered behind to wait for Jake to finish. He was still hunched over his notebook, scribbling with the kind of intensity that suggested he'd forgotten to breathe. Lilith picked up a crisp, veined, and impossibly perfect leaf. She played with it between her fingers, each twirl bringing up a different thought about everything that had happened since her birthday.

She lifted her gaze to the boys. "Random question: are most students here from gifted families? Or are there more clueless ones like me who still think they stepped into a weird dream?"

Jake grinned, straightening his back and finally tucking his notebook into his backpack. "Clueless? You know a ton," he said with a shrug. "But to answer you, I would say it's about half and half."

"Really? Half and half? Do kids from gifted parents choose not to accept their gift then? So the gods are always looking for new people to gift?"

"Mmm. Not really. It's hard to refuse your gift if your parents are gifted because we all grow up with this whole world around us. But lots of gifted people don't end up having children or even getting married. Plus population growth and all—it would only make sense the gods need more help, I guess?"

"Shhh," Arthur muttered, his sharp gaze snapping toward the forest's edge.

"Something wrong?" Lilith whispered, her leaf fluttering to the ground. Before he answered, five students emerged from the tree line. Their footsteps were casual, but their faces were anything but friendly.

The boy in front sneered. "Stupid thing. Stupid and disgusting," he muttered, loud enough to sting. "Wish we could stay and watch." He smirked. Jake winced in response—Lilith didn't have his empathy skill, but even she could tell something was off.

"We can come back later," a girl beside him added with a grin.

"Are you stupid too? Of course we're coming back," the first boy snapped.

Lilith, Arthur, and Jake stayed quiet as the group faded away toward the main building while discussing their schedules. It took a couple of seconds before Jake let out a shaky breath. "That's not good," he said with a grimace. "I think I'm gonna hurl. That dude's aura was—yuck." Jake shook out his arms, as if flinging off the bad energy before zipping up his backpack.

Arthur, on the other hand, watched the other students vanish from view before moving at all. A Ranger habit, Lilith had learned. And a good thing too. If she were the one responsible for noticing danger, their team would always be in trouble.

"Wait—did you hear that?" A faint sound threaded through the silence. Lilith cocked her head toward the forest.

"Hear what?" Arthur asked, angling his ear to the same area.

"I don't hear anything." Jake shrugged. "But," he paused. "I sense fear." A worried line creased his brow.

"Something isn't right." Lilith broke into a run, her feet pounding the ground as she bolted away.

"Lilith, where are you going?" Arthur yelled, racing after her.

"Help! Heeelp!" a high-pitched voice echoed louder with each step.

"We have to help!" Lilith hollered between gasps. Arthur and Jake exchanged a worried look but stayed close behind.

"All I hear are grunts," Arthur shouted, but he kept pace.

"I can feel it—the terror," Jake said, stumbling behind Lilith and Arthur.

"Where is she?!" Lilith skidded to a halt at a jagged cliff's edge.

"Is this Forever Falls?" Arthur murmured, eyeing the shards tumbling down the black abyss below. Sharp, gleaming slivers sparkled like broken mirrors.

"More like Blender Falls," Lilith blurted, legs trembling at the sight. "A waterfall of mirror shards, really? That shouldn't be anywhere near a school."

Arthur's mouth pressed into a grim line. "Those idiots must've messed it up with a spell. Last time I was here, it was just an ordinary endless waterfall." He stretched his neck, scanning the twisted chasm.

"Heeelp!" the voice cried out again, as if someone had shouted right in their faces, even though they couldn't see anyone.

Arthur tensed, electricity crackling between his fingers. "Watch out!"

Lilith whipped around, eyes darting everywhere. "For what?"

"Guys?" Jake's voice shook. A tear rolled down his cheek as he pointed down the cliff. Arthur and Lilith peeked over the edge. An Acephali hung from a narrow branch by one arm, her body streaked with cuts. With her other arm, she clutched a cloth-wrapped bundle so tightly her knuckles blanched.

"We're coming!" Lilith shouted, panic scraping up her throat.

Beside her, Arthur's electricity fizzled out. "Hills, we need a portal under the Acephali," he called sharply, but Jake stood frozen.

"Jake!" Lilith grabbed his shoulders and shook him hard. Nothing. "The blocker—" She thrust her hand into his jacket pocket, found the band, and wrapped it around his wrist. Jake dropped to his knees, gasping as a sob broke loose.

"A portal, now," Arthur barked.

"Jake?" Lilith knelt beside him, meeting his gaze. "We need you."

Jake blinked, voice raw. "P-portal. Yes."

A sharp crack snapped Lilith's attention back to the edge. The branch was giving in.

"Drop the bundle. Both hands on the branch!" Arthur shouted.

"NO!" the Acephali shrieked, panic shredding her voice.

Lilith shook her head. "Jake, now!"

Jake nodded, summoning a glowing lyre from his mark. A swirling portal yawned open beneath the Acephali, and its twin unfurled next to Lilith.

"Let go!" Lilith urged.

"Bad humans!" the Acephali growled, clutching the bundle as if its whole world hung by a thread. A spray of mirror shards burst against her shoulders, and she cried out in pain. Her grip faltered, just for a second.

The bundle slipped and vanished into the portal.

"Nooo!" the Acephali howled, diving off the branch and into the portal below.

A heartbeat later, the bundle shot out of the second portal. Lilith lunged for it, arms outstretched. It slammed into her arms, heavier than she expected. "Oof!" Lilith staggered back, arms burning, and hauled it clear of the portal just before the Acephali crashed through and hit the ground hard.

"Baby! Baby!" The Acephali scrabbled at the dirt in panic, digging like the ground had swallowed it.

"Here!" The weight tugged at Lilith's arms as she set the heavy bundle down gently. "We're trying to help."

"T-thank...you," the Acephali rasped, trembling as she pulled the bundle close. "The ones before...bad. Hurt Rose and baby."

Baby? The bundle! Lilith exhaled, wiping sweat from her brow. "We're not bad, I promise. Can we take you to the infirmary?"

"You understand Rose?" the creature asked, blinking.

Lilith frowned. "You mean... you? Your name is Rose?"

"Lilith?" Arthur called, stepping closer. "A little translation here? Jake and I can only hear... growls."

"Yeah," Jake muttered. "You're the only one who understands Acephalese right now."

"Acephalese? Oooh." Lilith's eyes widened, like a lightbulb had gone on. Her Hyperpolyglotism skill. "Sorry. This is Rose, and that," she added gently, "I think it's her baby. We really should get them to the infirmary."

Arthur's jaw tightened. He took in the face set in Rose's chest, the bundle locked in her oversized hands, and the injuries mottling her skin. Only then did he step in, as if she'd passed a silent safety check. "Yes, we should. May I?" he asked, voice steady.

Rose nodded. Arthur offered his shoulder without fully wrapping an arm around her, letting her settle her weight before he moved. "Thank... you," Rose mumbled, though only Lilith understood.

"You'll be okay, Rose. I'm Lilith, this is Arthur, and that's Jake." She gestured to her teammates. "Ready?" Jake nodded and opened another portal, this time leading them straight to the infirmary.

"Oh dear, oh dear!" Professor Thomas exclaimed, rushing over. "What happened here?" Her eyes swept over Rose and then the three of them.

"We're fine," Lilith said, helping Rose onto a bed. "She's the only one who's hurt."

"Oh! Then shoo, shoo." Professor Thomas flapped her hands. "You three, wait outside. I'll get Ezra after I deal with this dreadful mess of wounds," she added, pointing to the hallway.

"Principal Stewart?" Lilith's stomach dropped. How did she keep getting into trouble without even realizing it? Jake must've noticed she was spiraling, because he nudged her with his elbow and offered a gentle smile as they slumped onto the bench beside the infirmary door.

"You did good, Fletcher," Arthur said quietly, his tone uncharacteristically soft.

Maybe the Oracle was onto something, she thought. Maybe she did need Arthur and Jake if she was going to face whatever came next. She'd spent her whole life believing she had to fix everything on her own. But maybe, just maybe, letting someone else help wasn't such a bad idea.

CHAPTER SIXTEEN

TRAIN WRECK

P rincipal Stewart appeared in the hallway outside the infirmary with an unreadable expression and a presence that made the space feel smaller. His gaze flicked to each of them as if taking inventory. Professor Lewis walked beside him.

Lilith gulped, her chest still tight despite Jake and Arthur's earlier reassurance.

"Are you okay?" Jake asked, barely audible.

Lilith nodded, or tried to. It came out as a strange mix of a nod and a shrug.

"There is nothing to worry about," Arthur said, just loud enough for her and Jake to hear.

Then he stood, greeted the professors, and calmly explained what they had overheard after Teams 101: the students near the forest, the voices by the falls, Rose hanging over the cliff, injured and clinging to a branch.

Arthur spoke without a tremor in his voice, as if he were reporting oatmeal for breakfast. The more he spoke, the deeper Professor Lewis's frown became.

If Lilith hadn't grown used to Arthur, she might've sworn he was a robot. No expression. No anger. No fear. Nothing showed on the surface.

"This is far more serious than a prank," Principal Stewart said, frustration holding tight beneath his calm tone.

Professor Lewis pinched the bridge of his nose. "Maddening," he muttered. "We need to look into this, Ezra."

Principal Stewart nodded once and drew a long breath. "You three are free to go."

Lilith didn't move right away, waiting for the "*but.*" Weirdly, none came. So she followed the boys after Jake tugged her jacket.

It should not have felt like an ordinary day. But somehow, the Academy kept moving, and Lilith was expected to move with it.

Classes continued.

Assignments piled up.

The lump in her throat stayed.

In the weeks that followed, she couldn't shake the image of Rose wounded and shaking, or the thought of those students laughing like hurting someone was fine. Worse, like it was funny.

As a first-year, she barely had time to breathe, but life dragged her forward anyway. The Academy was strange for more than the workload or the unusual subjects. Classes blended students from every grade, grouped by skill instead of age, so Lilith ended up alongside advanced students in courses like Hyperpolyglotism III while trying to catch up in basic lessons such as Intro to Mythological History. On the bright side, the more teleportation classes she had, the better she got at it.

"Lilith!" Jake squealed as she arrived at Nature Manipulation. It was their last session before first-quarter exams.

Relief washed through her at the sight of him. Not just because Jake could explain a lesson when her brain felt like it might melt, or because he was helping her figure out how to talk to the Fates. It was simpler than that. Jake saw her as she was. No masks. No excuses. Just Lilith. And not having to pretend all the time was not only new, but freeing.

"Today, we will learn about *mugwort*," Professor Thomas announced, twirling across the room and holding up a flask. "Did you know that if you mix it with mint, it acts as a repellent?"

"Can it repel my Ancient Greek Civ class?" Lilith groaned to Jake, thunking her forehead lightly against her textbook.

Jake snickered, and she sighed—she loathed memorizing cities, borders, alliances, and dates.

"Did you just laugh at my misery?" she teased.

"Maybe," he whispered, and they both chuckled.

"Oh, check this out." Jake slid a book toward her, barely containing his grin. A newspaper clipping stuck out near the middle.

"I found something for your ritual," he whispered. "Go on. Read it."

SIRENS STRIKE AGAIN: OHIO TRAIN DERAILMENT RAISES ALARM

Second siren incident in less than a month sparks fears

By Ronnie Glenn | The Delphi Chronicle

In a chilling turn of events, a siren reportedly targeted a passenger train in Ohio last night, endangering lives outside the Veil of Illusion. Witnesses described an unearthly melody slicing through the dark, luring passengers toward disaster before the remaining cars could topple off the tracks.

This marks the second suspected siren strike in less than a month, prompting concern that these attacks are not isolated.

Last month, a similar derailment attempt sent shockwaves through the region, not only for the devastation it nearly caused but for what it revealed. When the train struck unstable soil, the impact exposed a hidden network of Fire Atrium Roots—rare, volatile, and still poorly understood. Coincidence... or connection?

As Ohio remains on edge, one question looms:

Are more strikes coming? *Updates to follow.*

"Mermaids... on a train?" Lilith whispered, confused. She'd always thought those things lived in the sea, singing to sailors and luring them to their doom.

"Sirens, not mermaids," Jake corrected. "Big difference—sirens have wings. Anyway, I'm thinking we could go there and scavenge for a siren feather."

"That's... genius," she said, eyes lighting up.

"Genius would be if you two focused on class," Professor Thomas cut in, her voice sharp but not unkind. Lilith's cheeks burned as a few heads turned in their direction.

"Sorry," she mumbled, sinking in her seat.

The lesson wrapped up soon enough, and as they left the classroom, Jake dragged Lilith aside, excitement barely contained. "I really think this could work! But we need to find a way to get a permission slip," he continued eagerly.

Lilith frowned. "Can't we just ask Professor Lewis to let us go there to look for the feathers for my ritual?"

"Staff can't exactly sanction a random 'siren-feather hunt,' and I doubt he'd approve the Fates ritual," Jake replied.

"I guess..." The bell rang and Lilith rolled her eyes. "I have to run. I've got two more classes before my next break. But we can meet later and bounce ideas?"

"Sounds good." Jake waved as they split up in the hallway.

Greek Civ dragged on endlessly, a dull blur of information she knew she'd forget. But the following class, Life Powder Manipulation I, was the opposite—hands-on and strangely fascinating. At least as long as she didn't have to collect Life Powder from anyone.

Sculpting the dust with her imagination was actually fun: challenging, but satisfying, if she didn't factor in the whole life-versus-death part. When the lesson finally ended, Lilith lingered, carefully stacking her materials. Her fingers fumbled, and her book slipped, hitting the floor with a thud. The siren article caught a draft and spiraled ahead.

"Got it," Adrien said, snatching the paper. Lilith blinked. She'd almost forgotten he was in this class. Adrien was always surrounded by other students, so they didn't talk much.

"Thanks," she said, sliding her book into her backpack and holding out her hand for the clipping.

Adrien's eyes flicked over the headline. "Siren feathers?" he asked, like he already knew that wasn't homework. He arched an eyebrow. "You're really trying to do that ritual, aren't you?"

"I'm out of options," she said, impressed he'd clocked it from a siren article. "The only real snag is getting a permission slip."

Adrien's mouth curved into a mischievous grin. "I can get you one."

"You can?" Her eyes narrowed.

"Sure, but I want in," he said nonchalantly.

"Why?" Lilith frowned.

"You never know what you'll find out there. I like discovering things," he said with a shrug. "Deal?"

"I guess?" Lilith said, still unsure. "How do we get the slip?"

"Leave that to me. See you in the main lobby in an hour." Adrien gave a quick wave before hurrying off.

Lilith scribbled quick notes to Jake and Arthur through her map, updating them about Adrien and the slip. Then she stuffed the map in her pocket and eyed her backpack. She'd better stop by her room to unload some weight before heading to the lobby. She probably should have reviewed her notes about the foundational tales of gods, heroes, and monsters, but her mind couldn't stop going back to the article. She had read that piece of paper about twenty times by the time her phone rang. It was Dad. Her forehead creased before she answered. They probably talked more often now than when she had actually lived with him.

She answered, keeping her tone light. She told him about calculus, while he told her about a *"welcome back plan"* he, Meghan, and Amy were putting together for when she came home for break. Lilith's hearing went foggy. Her dad's voice kept going, but the words blurred together. Since when did he make plans *for* her? She was used to the standard *if I have time* excuse for everything, always.

"...Sound good?" Nicholas asked.

Lilith blinked hard. What was he even talking about? "Mm-hmm. Yeah," she answered, a beat too fast.

After nearly half an hour, a muffled voice sounded on his end. "Dr. Fletcher, you're needed in Room 379." He sighed. "Gotta go, bud. We'll talk soon."

"Yeah," she said. "Bye, Dad."

Lilith stared at the wall for a beat before grabbing her things and heading toward the main lobby. Her thoughts drifted. *Could Adrien really pull this off? And even if he did, would they find a feather at all?* She inhaled deeply, pushing the thought aside as she hurried down the corridor.

"Are you serious?" Jake's voice made her turn just as he caught up with her by the map fountain. He was practically glowing. "How did you even get the slip?" he asked, almost bouncing.

"It was Adrien, not me," Lilith corrected.

"Same thing!" He grinned like Amy getting extra screen time from Mcghan. "Oh, change of subject... Those jerks who hurt Rose finally got detention. The investigation took forever, but it worked out."

Lilith's shoulders slumped. "Detention's nothing for what they did," she barked.

"Hey, rookies," Adrien's voice cut in. He strode over, waving a small paper and a couple of cloth pouches. "I've got something you want. Let's fill it out." He looked annoyingly pleased with himself.

Jake stared at the slip in awe. "You have to teach me how you get those."

Adrien smirked. "No problem, but you owe me more of that healing ointment," he said with a wink, handing the paper over to Jake.

"A thousand times yes," Jake replied, fixing his glasses and scanning the slip. "Volunteer supply run. Clever! How did you even know the infirmary needed mushrooms?"

"I have my contacts." Adrien shrugged, then reached for the slip and scrawled their names on the paper. "Done."

"Um... You forgot Arthur's name," Jake said slowly.

Adrien rolled his eyes. "He's not even here. I figured His Royal Highness wasn't interested. No offense, but he's so..." He made a face, as if he was searching for the word.

"So...?" Arthur strode up.

Adrien exhaled like the universe had personally inconvenienced him. "Whatever." He added Arthur's name with a sharp flourish and flicked the slip into the map fountain. The paper dissolved on contact, like it was made of cotton candy. The water swirled, gathering into a glowing orb above the basin, and bright letters flared to life across its surface. OHIO pulsed once. Beneath it, their names appeared in neat, floating script.

Jake caught Lilith's wide-eyed stare and grinned. He pointed to a white-lit circle set into the floor. "This ring lets us teleport in and out with official permission." He inhaled like he'd been holding it in. "This is gonna be so much fun!"

"Shall we?" Arthur said, reaching for Lilith and Jake's wrists.

But when Jake turned to Adrien, Adrien stepped away and scoffed. "No one teleports me. I can do it myself," he said, stepping into the circle and vanishing in a flash of blue.

"And I'm the Royal Highness?" Arthur rolled his eyes. "Okay, ready?"

Lilith and Jake nodded. Arthur tightened his grip, and the world tilted. Lilith's fingers tingled as a soft blue glow swallowed them. She braced for dizziness. None came. Maybe those Teleportation lessons were finally paying off. An instant later, the Academy walls had vanished, replaced by twisted train wreckage, torn tracks, and the sharp scent of metal and oil.

"Let's get to work," Arthur said.

"Wait, where's Adrien?" Jake scanned the area. "Did he mess up his jump?"

"I'm not a babysitter." Arthur bent to examine the grass beneath a torn sheet of metal.

"Arthur!" Lilith scolded.

"Oh, wait, I just got a message from Adrien," Jake said, glancing up from his phone. "He said he'll meet us here in an hour."

Arthur sighed. "Of course he will." He straightened and nudged a broken panel aside. "Then we use the hour. We can at least bag some mushrooms for our little cover story." He plucked a cluster and tucked it into a pouch at his belt.

Jake puffed up his chest. "Well, I'm not waiting to start searching." He conjured a small glowing sun-arrow and fired it skyward. "This is so cool. Let's make these siren feathers glint—I mean, if any are lying around."

"Nice move, Hills," Arthur commented, and Jake beamed.

"Isn't it weird to have a bunch of kids wandering around a wreck? What if non-gifted humans see us?" Lilith asked, stepping over debris.

"We're under the Veil of Illusion, Fletcher," Arthur reminded her. "Humans will see animals... or nothing at all, depending on the veil's choice."

"The veil. Right," Lilith repeated. She would never get used to that, would she?

Jake nocked another arrow and fired. The glowing projectile soared, bursting open like a flare. Light rippled outward, peeling back the shadows and illuminating the wreckage for a couple of seconds.

It was time to find a siren feather.

CHAPTER SEVENTEEN

ROGUE ATTACK

For about forty minutes, they lifted metal sheets, collected mushrooms, and mistook more glints of broken glass for feathers than Lilith could count. Then Jake yelped from the far side of the railroad tracks. "Wowie, wowie, wow!"

"No way!" she called back. "You're pranking me." Her boots crunched over the gravel as he waved something that caught the light overhead.

"We did it! We actually did it!" Jake bounced while Arthur stood beside him, looking annoyingly unsurprised.

Lilith stepped over the rails, ready to celebrate, when blue light flared before she could reach them. Adrien appeared right in her path. "We gotta go!" he rasped, bent over, one hand clamped to his stomach. "They attacked me. They're coming."

"What? Who?" Jake asked, shoving the shimmering object into his pocket.

"Now," Adrien rasped, trying and failing to stand upright. "Rogues."

"How many?" Arthur stepped in front of them, gaze sweeping the surroundings. He clocked the high ground, the narrow gaps between the bushes, and the way the grass lay flattened near the tracks.

"Not sure," Adrien wheezed as Lilith grabbed his arm to steady him. "At least two. Definitely advanced."

Storm clouds boiled overhead. Arthur's gaze snapped up, electricity prickling at his fingertips as thunder rumbled.

"Arthur, we can't start a fight. You know the rules," Jake pleaded. "Let's just get out of here."

"This isn't me," Arthur said, his jaw setting. "Someone else has weather control." He raised his hands, throwing a shield above the group.

Beside her, Adrien fumbled at the pendant at his neck and poured a pinch of Life Powder into his palm. Lilith bit her lip and traced her mark. Powder stirred from her pendant, lifting in a faint spiral beneath her chin like she knew what she was doing. She didn't. Defensive Arts & Tactical Combat had taught them the basics and even thrown students into practice scenarios, but Lilith had never been in a real fight. *A confident face is half the battle*, her combat teacher's voice echoed in her mind.

"Thank the Olympians," Jake blurted, his head snapping left. "Teachers!"

Blue light split the air again, and three teachers appeared as Arthur lowered the shield.

"You kids all right?" Professor Lewis asked. They nodded. "Then we're leaving," he said.

Professor Homolka and Professor Goldsmith moved into position, forming a triangle around the students.

"Now," Professor Lewis called. Light surged up again and the wreckage vanished, replaced by the Academy's lobby in a single blink. Professor Goldsmith immediately swept a hand over the permission circle next to their feet. It flared red, then sank into the floor.

"What in Olympus happened out there?" Professor Lewis's gaze landed on Lilith.

"Uh—" Lilith stammered.

"We volunteered to gather mushrooms," Arthur cut in.

"You—volunteered?" Professor Goldsmith's suspicion settled on Arthur, like the concept didn't fit him.

"We did," Lilith confirmed, pulling the mushroom-filled sack from her belt pouch like proof. Professor Lewis's eyes dropped to it, then lifted again. Unblinking.

Adrien croaked, "I jumped first and came down in the wrong place." The professors exchanged a quick look, as if each new detail made the story sound less like a supply run and more like a cover-up.

"He messaged that he was fine, though," Arthur said. His gaze flicked once to Adrien, then back to Lewis. "But by the time he reached us, he was injured and said rogues were after him. I raised a shield and held position until staff arrived," he finished.

"They were asking for my teammates," Adrien added, wincing as he clutched his side. "Please. Check on them." His usual swagger was gone.

Professor Lewis nodded once. Maybe urgency had finally outweighed suspicion. "All right. You four, with me. Infirmary." Then his gaze cut to Goldsmith. "Is the portal sealed?"

"Yes. Locked down," Professor Goldsmith confirmed.

"Good," Professor Lewis said. He turned to Homolka. "You and Goldsmith, check on Hannah Jones and Kami Mills. Make sure they're safe."

Homolka and Goldsmith nodded. Professor Lewis guided them to the infirmary, where Professor Thomas wasted no time tending to Adrien.

"How did the teachers even find us?" Lilith whispered from the corner of the room. "Were they watching? Do they know—"

Arthur's eyes flicked to the door, then the windows, then back to Adrien. "They weren't watching. Slip locations are warded." His voice stayed calm, but his posture didn't. "If rogues breach the spell, the Academy gets alerted."

Lilith glanced at Jake. He'd been unusually quiet. She checked his wrist, the empathy blocker still on. "You okay?" she asked, leaning closer.

"Yeah. It's just..." He hesitated. "Why go after Kami and Hannah? Rogues risking a breach for two apprentices who weren't even there... that doesn't make sense."

"It doesn't," Arthur said, finally turning. His gaze sharpened. "And Fjeld doesn't misjump."

Jake's lips flattened. "None of this fits."

Lilith forced a thin shrug, like she could shrug the dread off. "Maybe they crossed the wrong person," she said, then hesitated.

"There we go," Professor Thomas told Adrien briskly. "You'll be fine." She looked toward Professor Lewis. "May we speak?" Then she ushered the professors outside.

The door clicked shut. As soon as the students were alone, Lilith went over to Adrien's bedside. "You all right?"

"I'll recover," he said with a grimace.

"So how did you end up in the wrong spot?" Arthur asked, no warm-up.

Adrien exhaled. "It wasn't an accident. I jumped to the other train-wreck site first."

"Why?" Jake asked, scratching his forehead.

"That siren article," Adrien said, nodding toward Lilith. "It mentioned Fire Atrium Roots."

Jake went pale. "Those are restricted at the Academy."

"Exactly," Adrien said flatly. "Which is why I didn't want anyone tagging along. Not when I needed to grab some for a little... project."

"And then the rogues found you?" Lilith narrowed her eyes. "Were they after the roots? Did you toss Hannah and Kami into the story to throw the professors off?"

Adrien's gaze dropped. "No." His voice lowered, the bravado thinning. "It was really weird. I didn't make it up. I got hit from behind. Hard." He swallowed. "First, a guy kept demanding to know where the rest of my team was." His jaw tightened. "Then a woman showed up and said if I cooperated, they might let me walk away." He sucked in a breath. "I tried to fight, but they didn't fight fair, and it happened so fast." His voice caught, just slightly. "I wasn't... ready." He dragged a hand through his hair. "When they started arguing, I took the second I had and jumped to you." He looked up, eyes suddenly sharp. "I don't know what they wanted with my team, but it can't be to give them a hug."

Before they could say more, Professor Thomas reentered the room and jerked her head toward the door. "All right. Everyone out."

For three days, unease thickened the Academy halls. Whispers slithered from corridor to corridor, speculation multiplying as if it fed on silence. Had rogues broken in? Had the portals failed? For Olympus's sake, it happened in Ohio, yet somehow the Academy had already invented a hundred versions of it.

On the third day, Lilith was taking her seat in Life Powder Manipulation I when Adrien finally showed up after being stuck in the infirmary, and the rumor mill went feral.

"Oh, Adrien," Professor Chronus said with a calm, courteous smile. "You're welcome to take the rest of the week off if you need to." He stroked his impeccably groomed mustache.

Adrien straightened, rolling his shoulders back. "I'm fine, Professor," he said. "Didn't you say I needed to help them with the floating maneuver?"

Professor Chronus chuckled. "Yes, but I assumed you'd still be recovering today... after the incident."

The room stilled. Then gasps and whispers snapped through the class, hushed voices ricocheting from desk to desk, but Adrien smirked. "Nah. I'm good. Ready whenever you are."

Lilith barely heard the rest. The moment the incident was mentioned, a knot tightened in her stomach. Ever since they came back from Ohio, she couldn't shake the feeling that hunting ritual ingredients had been reckless. Selfish, even. Not that she had much of a choice from now on. Every portal was locked, and field trips were off the table, which meant her chances of getting the missing hair and scale were pretty much zero. But even if they hadn't been trapped at the Academy, the danger was real now. *Was it fair to ask her friends to keep helping?*

She stared blankly ahead, Chronus's lecture dissolving into static. Adrien demonstrated the maneuver, students drifting upward in neat little lifts, but she barely registered any of it.

When class ended, the room buzzed with movement. Students swarmed Adrien, hungry for details, while Lilith slipped away to meet Jake in the Zeus Wing common area. The weight in her chest only grew with each step. *How could she get out of the Fates' bond without putting anyone in danger?*

"Lilith?" Jake's voice cut through her haze.

"Huh?" she murmured.

"Everything all right?" he asked gently.

Lilith managed a half shrug. "I guess."

Jake opened his jacket like a street vendor with contraband. "I think you should keep this." He pulled out a black feather.

Lilith frowned. "Did it... change colors?"

"That was my search spell," Jake said. "Siren feathers shift like chameleons, only worse. That's what makes them so hard to track." He slid his hand behind it. "Watch." The feather rippled, the center turning the color of his skin while the ends blended into his jacket. "Careful not to lose it," he said, holding it out.

Lilith reached for it, and the moment her fingers brushed the quill, her eyes widened. It was softer than Amy's treasured bunny, softer even than her mom's old stuffed penguin. Softer than anything she'd ever touched.

"It's pretty cool, huh?" Jake grinned. "Okay, I've got news."

Lilith tucked the feather into her jacket and looked back at him. "Yeah?"

"You and Arthur are enrolling in Intro to Mythical Creatures," Jake said, mischief bright in his eyes.

Lilith tipped her head. "Another class? Why do you want us in that?"

"Because they do a live Minotaur encounter at the end of the year. If we can't find another option before then, it's a solid backup plan."

"That's perfect," she said, chin high. It couldn't get any safer than this, not if it was part of class. "And you don't want to sign up too?"

"I kinda..." He winced. "Let's just say Professor Moonlit banned me from the minotaur practical. Possibly from her entire existence."

Lilith gasped. "You can't say that and not tell me."

He coughed into his sleeve. "I absolutely can." Then he perked up, like a subject change could erase the mystery. "Anyway, once you're in the encounter, you can snag a minotaur hair. Then voilà, another ingredient down."

Lilith pressed her lips together, pretending to think hard. "Fine. But if curiosity kills me, I'm haunting you."

He grinned. "We still need the python scale, though," he said, standing so they could head out.

"Right. Could we find a python scale around here? Somewhere safe? Maybe near the forest, under the protective barrier?" Lilith asked, falling into step beside him.

Jake shook his head. "Not just any snake. It has to be descended from the Delphic python." He smirked. "Which is also why you really need to learn more about mythical creatures."

"Hey! Are you mocking me?" Lilith teased, bumping him with her shoulder.

"Absolutely not. I'm respectfully suggesting our team leader study the creatures that might eat us," he said with a bow.

Lilith slowed. "I'll never understand why I'm the team leader. You or Arthur would be so much better at it. I barely understand anything here."

Jake looked genuinely thrown. "What are you talking about? We picked you."

Lilith stared at him. "Wait. It wasn't a Looper thing? I thought Adrien was the leader of his team, so I figured..." She trailed off. "Why would you two pick me?"

He shrugged like it was obvious. "There's no rule saying Loopers have to be the leaders. And I can't speak for Arthur, but from the moment we met under that tree, I just knew." His grin turned softer. "Call it a gut feeling."

Lilith's face reddened. Compliments still felt like a language she hadn't learned, except from Meghan or Amy, which didn't count because they were family. She cleared her throat and mumbled a quick thanks, then hurried ahead before she could blush herself into a puddle. "Oh, I saw Adrien earlier," she added, too quickly. "He looks better. And thanks to Professor Chronus, the whole class knows rogues attacked him."

Jake snorted. "It's not just your class. He's been selling his heroic saga to anyone with ears." He chuckled. "Come on. Let's meet Arthur and get you two enrolled before he starts training and disappears."

A steadier sense of purpose settled in Lilith's chest. They had a plan that sounded safe enough. They had each other. And with every small win—a siren feather, a minotaur hair on the horizon—they were inching closer to breaking free of the Fates' bond.

CHAPTER EIGHTEEN

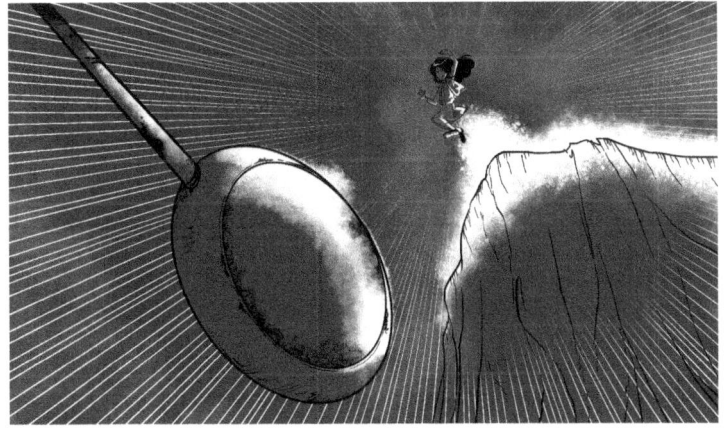

THE DEPTHS OF THUNDER

S ome days were short, some were long, but that day was endless. Lilith had been counting the minutes until bed, even though she still had hours to go. After finally enrolling in the long-awaited Intro to Mythical Creatures, surviving two grueling classes, and enduring a pop quiz in Nature Manipulation, her brain felt like mush. All she wanted was to call Amy, grab a snack, and collapse in bed until the next morning.

Lilith stuffed her belongings into her backpack as Professor Thomas raised a delicate, gold-rimmed teacup patterned with tiny flowers.

"Have a wonderful rest of your day, everyone," the professor said warmly. Then, almost as an afterthought, she added, "Oh, and don't mind the sweep spells being cast today. They can't hurt a fly." She dismissed the class with a serene smile.

Students flooded toward the door, and Lilith would have gladly followed if Jake hadn't gone stiff beside her. "Um, e-excuse me, Professor Thomas?"

"Yes, dear?" she replied, taking another sip.

"Did you say... sweep spells?"

Professor Thomas smiled. "Yes, dear. After the rogue incident, we decided to sweep dorms, common areas, and classrooms. For your protection, of course. Nothing to worry about."

Jake's face drained of color. "Thanks," he croaked, then grabbed Lilith's sleeve and practically yanked her into the hallway.

"What's going on?" Lilith asked, stumbling to keep up.

"We're in trouble. Deep trouble," Jake whispered, hauling her faster. "Like, heads-rolling trouble. We have to get your stuff out of your room before they find it."

"Stuff—oh." Lilith's stomach dropped. The word tasted like doom.

"Move, move," Jake hissed, breaking into a sprint.

They tore through the hallways, dodging students until they reached Pi Commons.

"Go. I'll keep watch," Jake ordered, scanning the corridor.

Lilith rushed inside. Backpack, box. Desk drawer, everything. Ritual items, herbs, pages scribbled with notes—she scooped it all up before peeking out. "Got it," she whispered. "Now what?"

Jake's eyes darted down the hall. A professor stood only a few doors away. "I don't know. We're doomed," he mouthed, wiping his brow.

"Snap out of it," Lilith said, sharp and low, and they tore down the last corridor toward the sharp air and wide sky of the Diplomatic Terrace.

"You're here!" Jake yelled, catching sight of Arthur practicing alone at the far end.

"Perfect timing," Lilith panted when they got closer. "We need to talk, now."

Arthur raised an eyebrow. "Something up?"

"The teachers are casting sweep spells," Jake blurted. "We have to put you-know-what away."

Arthur's expression sharpened. "I see." He turned on his heel. "I know a spot. Trust me."

Jake and Lilith exchanged a look. "Wait. Where are you going? That's back toward Zeus Wing. Did I not mention they're sweeping it right now?"

Arthur shot him a deadpan look. "Stop talking and follow me."

Jake's anxiety mounted with every step. Lilith could almost feel his heartbeat in the air. Arthur rushed through the corridors until they got to a narrow library entrance.

Lilith frowned. She hadn't noticed it before. Not that she'd seen even a fraction of the Academy, the place was ridiculously huge, but this door was tucked beside the quiet little corner where she and Jake always sat to devour books and chat.

Inside, the small library looked deserted, dim lighting stretching long shadows across the shelves, each etched with lightning symbols.

"They'll still sweep the library," Jake whispered, his voice tipping toward frantic. "Maybe we should ditch everything."

"I..." Lilith tightened her grip on her backpack strap. *Ditch everything?* She was so close to being ready for the ritual... She'd rather get into trouble. "You can go, Jake. If I'm caught, I won't tell anyone you were involved," she added, softer, like a promise.

"Shh." Arthur lifted a finger to his lips like an order. "You two are driving me insane. Just zip it and follow me."

Jake glanced over his shoulder, at Lilith and at the towering shelves before he adjusted his glasses and followed. Arthur led them deeper, weaving between rows with practiced ease, like he'd walked this route a hundred times. Four other shelves down, he turned left. Lilith nearly ran into his back when he stopped in front of a solid stone wall.

Arthur's wrist crackled with electricity as he pressed his palm into one of the lightning-shaped carvings in the wall, feeding it power. The symbol flared, glowing an eerie blue. Then, with a low creak, a section of marble floor groaned open, revealing a hidden passage.

Jake gaped. "How did I not know about this?" he whispered, horrified, like missing one hidden door meant he'd failed some nonexistent test.

"Come," Arthur called, already stepping into the opening.

A flight of stairs spiraled downward into darkness. Lilith paused at the threshold, heart racing. That was the kind of place Lilith would shout at the actors not to go into when she watched a horror movie—but she went in anyway. The air thickened with the scent of damp stone. At the bottom, the entrance closed, leaving the room pitch black until Arthur summoned a crackling bolt of lightning. He flung it upward. Energy arced across the ceiling, igniting clusters of lights one by one. Shadows retreated, revealing a vast chamber.

"Whoa," Jake breathed. His eyes sparkled with childlike wonder. "What... What is this place?"

Arthur smirked. "There are some advantages to being an Owens. My grandfather used to tell stories about a secret room he and his friends practiced spells in." He glanced around, almost casual. "So I found it. I come here a lot."

Jake stared up at the enchanted ceiling. "So the rumors about Zeus's hidden room are... true? Like, really true?"

Arthur spread his hands with a small flourish. "Yes, this is one of Harpocrates's hidden rooms. The Zeus Vault."

Lilith turned slowly, taking in the scale of it. Ancient stone stretched farther than it should have, lined with heavy wooden doors that promised who-knew-what. Dust clung to the corners, cobwebs veiling the edges, like the place had been waiting for years to be remembered.

"Your things will be safe here, Fletcher," Arthur said. "We could probably do the ritual here too. But listen. You can't tell anyone about this place. And... you can't get in without me because only Zeus apprentices can open the passage."

"Throw away the key," Lilith promised, dragging two fingers across her mouth.

"Same here." Jake raised a hand in mock oath.

Arthur nodded once, satisfied. "Good. Put your stuff there." He gestured to an old chest near the wall.

Jake took two steps closer. "Is this a Hush Chest? Just when I thought this place couldn't get any cooler!"

"Hush Chest?" Lilith ran her finger across the surface. A boy with one finger pressed over his lips was embossed on top. Harpocrates, she recognized. Hours of studying deities were finally paying off.

"Yep. I heard Professor Lewis has one in his chambers. Go on, put everything inside. I'll show you how it works! It's one of the most popular items crafted by Harpocrates. History says only one hundred were made, but some have been destroyed or vanished over time." Jake's words raced so fast it sounded like someone had hit the 3x speed button.

When she lifted the lid, the mark on her wrist pulsed once. The chest looked half the size inside. Maybe it was the padding, Lilith thought. She unzipped her backpack and transferred everything into the chest. Glass vials clicked against wood. Paper edges scraped. The siren feather slid in last, soft as a secret. The lid closed with a click.

"Watch this," Jake said, opening the chest himself.

It was empty.

Lilith clutched her head with both hands, her heart jumping. "Nobody else can open your version of the chest," Jake explained with a big smile. "It creates a new lock for whoever activates it."

She wished he had explained that before giving her a heart attack, but skeptical as she was, she opened it again to double-check. And all her things were inside this time, safe and sound. Relief hit first, sharp and dizzying. They did it. The ritual could still happen. She could still talk to the Fates to return her gift.

Then came a flicker of something she didn't know what to do with: the feeling of being included. But it didn't last long. Guilt followed close behind, like a hand on her throat. Arthur and Jake were risking trouble for her, helping her chase a way out. But the way out had a cost. If the ritual worked, she would return the Fates' gift and leave, which meant leaving them too. No more Jake's grin at breakfast, no more Arthur saying "trust me" like it was a rule of the universe.

The thought hit like ice. Then the other side of the choice flared up, just as ugly. Staying meant keeping the gift—becoming someone who was responsible for taking lives. She shut the lid a little harder than she meant to, like she could trap the thought inside. The fear of choosing wrong, of regretting it later, pressed hard against her ribs. *Was she running from the only place she'd started to fit?*

"Come on, we need to get back upstairs before curfew," Arthur said. "When the passage opens, it creates a veil until it closes again, so don't freak out if someone is nearby. No one will see us." Then he flipped the bolt-shaped lever again, opening the entrance above, spilling light down the staircase.

They climbed out one by one, checked the library, and slipped back between the shelves.

With sweep spells still in effect and portals locked down, the halls stayed jumpy, full of whispers about rogue intrusions. But the Zeus Vault slowly became their safe spot. They headed there whenever they could: after dinner, during breaks, even in the early mornings. Lilith learned the turns by heart, the way the air changed on the stairs, the rooms that smelled like dust and ozone. Her first move was always the same: check the chest. She knew it was ridiculous. Everything was protected. But she did it anyway.

Jake had his own habit too: whenever they were inside the Vault, he ran his fingers across the walls. After growing up hearing rumors about Harpocrates's secret rooms, actually standing inside made him wonder what else was hiding at the Academy. Lilith couldn't count the number of times he made Arthur retell the story of how his grandfather had found the room as a boy, and how Arthur had found it decades later and had been using it for the past year.

Jake treated the place like a puzzle, poking into corners and cataloging details as his fascination grew. Every visit showed them something new. Even Arthur discovered things he hadn't noticed before.

The Zeus Vault was basically a buried training wing, with rooms for combat drills, spell refinement, and maze-like corridors. They made good use of it too—luckily, gifted humans healed faster than ordinary humans. After so many scrapes, bruises, and sore muscles, Lilith would have been in serious trouble otherwise. While they had to tiptoe everywhere else, the Vault was where they planned, rested, talked, and trained. Time blurred past in exhaustion, discovery, and a quiet determination that didn't ask permission.

"Think we can train after Teams 101?" Lilith asked as they headed to class together.

"I'm free," Jake said.

"Same," Arthur replied.

A ripple of movement down the hall tugged at Lilith's attention. Students were stopping and whispering.

"Fletcher?" Arthur called, but she was already weaving through the crowd.

"What's going on?" Lilith asked, catching up to Ruby, a short brunette first-year slipping away from the throng, with Arthur and Jake close behind.

"Class is canceled," Ruby said with a shrug.

Lilith frowned. "Canceled? Why?"

Ruby shrugged again. "Something about Professor Lewis helping with the portals. But I can't complain because I could really use this time to review for my spells test. Gotta go, bye!" She darted off.

"If class is canceled, we could use the time to get some training too," Arthur suggested. "The minotaur lessons aren't far off."

"I'm so in!" Jake said, instantly brighter.

Lilith laughed. "Yes, please."

A boy was dozing over an open book at the first table of the Zeus Library—the first time Lilith had seen anyone there. She, Arthur, and Jake eased past him, quiet as thieves and slipped into the Vault without trouble. "Which room did we use last time?" Jake asked, glancing at a set of mirrors.

Arthur pointed. "The Deity Traps room."

Jake's eyes sparked. "Obstacle course today?"

Lilith groaned. She hated that one. It was her personal failure room because she had never completed it.

"Any other room but that one!" she tried.

"Come on, Fletcher, you can't avoid it forever," Arthur scolded.

"Fiiiine," she pouted, dropping her backpack near the wall.

They ran the course six or seven times. Arthur, of course, breezed through on his first attempt, annoyingly perfect. Lilith tilted her head, noticing Jake behind her on the rope.

"Focus, Fletcher, no looking back," Arthur called.

"Okay," Lilith mumbled, refocusing.

Zap. First ring. *Zap.* Second. A flicker of light, the whoosh of a swinging dummy, and dizziness crawled up her spine. She clipped the pendulum hard while Jake made it across, waving like he'd won a medal.

"Ugh, I can't do it! That third ring is impossible!" Lilith fumed, sprawled on the padded floor.

Jake wiped sweat from his forehead and checked the time. "I've got my next class in ten. Should we call it?"

Lilith scowled at the pendulum. "It's pointless anyway."

"It's not pointless. You can do it. You're just having trouble," Arthur said, arms folding. "Hills, go to your class. We'll stay."

Jake hesitated, then nodded. His gaze flicked to Lilith before heading out. "You'll get it," he encouraged.

"Catch your breath, Fletcher. I'll see Hills out. Be right back." He followed Jake out into the main chamber.

Lilith crossed her arms and closed her eyes. *Why was she the only one who couldn't do it? It wasn't like she had a secret ninja talent—but neither did Jake. And she had been doing just fine in*

Teams 101 and the obstacle courses from Defensive Arts & Tactical Combat. So, what was wrong with her?

"Ready to give it another try?" Arthur asked, re-entering the room.

"I just can't do it," she said, glaring at the dummy by the third ring.

Arthur rolled his eyes and offered her a hand. "Come on."

"Whatever." She took his hand with as much attitude as possible.

By the time she was up, the room blinked. She and Arthur were at the course's start. For a heartbeat she thought Arthur had teleported her, but they were facing an earlier version of Lilith, shoulders squared like she still believed she could win.

Lilith threw up her hands. "Are you *trying* to humiliate me?"

"We are learning," he said simply. "Do you remember when I kept messing up the bolt in the Elemental Arena? It happened because my feet weren't at the right angle. I didn't catch it until I studied myself and—wait! Look." He pointed.

Lilith squinted. "What?" She watched herself crash again.

Arthur's eyes sparked. He caught something she didn't. Without asking, he pulled them back in time again. "Here," he said. "Right before you hit the third ring. Watch your eyes."

Lilith stared. The pupils of her earlier self sharpened into cat-like slits, then snapped back. "What in the world?"

Arthur looked annoyingly pleased with himself, and the world snapped forward again. Back in the present, he flicked his fingers, darkness swallowing the room.

"What are you doing?" Lilith yelped.

"Try again," he said.

"The course? Are you nuts? It's too dark!"

"Just trust me. On you go," he insisted.

Lilith drew a long breath and stepped to the start. Her eyes narrowed—*it wasn't that dark, was it?* She could see pretty much everything in shades of gray. *Zap.* First ring. *Zap.* Second. The dummy whooshed past, but something was different. She wasn't dizzy this time.

Zap. She made it through the third ring. *Zap, zap.* Through the fourth and fifth, clean as air.

"I...did it?" she whispered, still in disbelief.

Arthur restored the light with a new bolt. "I knew we would figure it out," he said, like he'd solved a puzzle. "Drakon-sight."

Lilith tilted her head. "Drakon-who?" She touched the upper part of her cheek like she could feel it. "That's... a thing?"

"Think of it as a vision superpower," Arthur said. "All Nyx-gifted have it. It's basically their signature."

"Does that mean the second deity to gift me was Nyx?" A spark lit up in her chest.

He glanced at her like he was filing the fact away. "Nyx isn't the only deity who offers Drakon-sight. Plus Nyx-gifted people don't have Nature Manipulation skills. So no, you're not gifted by Nyx."

Her throat bobbed. "But I'm not a complete failure either." She had finally done the course, and she chose to cling to that victory.

"You're anything but," Arthur said, mouth twitching. "Now let's see if you can call your sight on purpose."

Lilith grinned, pulse racing. "Another round? Lights off?"

Arthur's smirk widened. "You're on. But don't think I'll take it easy on you. And next round, lights on."

"Sure, if you can beat me, you can bring light back again," she taunted.

CHAPTER NINETEEN

ECHOES OF THE PAST

L ilith had been fidgeting with a rubber band, her mind miles
away. That day marked eight months since her fourteenth
birthday. Time had slipped by in a way that felt unfair, like
someone kept stealing pages while she wasn't looking. Somewhere
along the way, classes had stopped feeling like classes. They started
feeling like reconnaissance. What to recognize. What to avoid.
What a creature part looked like when it wasn't sitting neatly on
a page. Intro to Mythical Creatures became one of her favorites
because it wasn't just study this anymore. It was: *don't mistake*

minotaur hair for a chimera tuft. Don't step wrong when a python can feel you through the floor. Don't forget that most creatures don't fight like humans.

The world wasn't trivia. It was a checklist her heartbeat could finally understand. And her Drakon-sight? She pushed through the skull-buzz and the sore eyes, forcing the skill to obey, calling it up on purpose and letting it go before it burned too deep. It became a tool she learned to control. Meghan used to joke Lilith could spot a needle in a haystack. But Drakon-sight was something else.

When the lights went out, the dark reorganized. Edges snapped into focus, motion slowed, and the swinging dummy stopped being a blur and became a path. Even in daylight, it lived beneath her normal vision, a second layer she was learning to call up. Moving objects left faint after-trails, as if her brain sketched where they had been and where they were headed next. Headaches and exhaustion aside, it was worth it. She could widen her sight until she caught everything at once, or narrow it until the world went quiet except for a single target. And sometimes, during combat drills, she could even spot apprentices who had turned invisible, not by calling out Life Powder, but by the soft heat-halo their bodies could not fully hide... unless they had mastered something harder.

The ritual was almost within reach. They had finally gotten Midas Elixir and a Life-Powder painting of the Fates. Only two impossible pieces remained: a minotaur's hair and a python's scale. Lilith could feel it too, in the way Jake's excitement spilled out of him like steam, and in the way Arthur had started checking corridors twice instead of once.

After class, Lilith threw herself onto her bed and stared at her phone, thumb circling the frayed seam of her mom's old penguin plush. Her phone buzzed. Meghan had sent a picture of Amy asleep on Lilith's bed. Somehow Amy looked so much older than the last time she had called—and that had only been a few days ago. Lilith sent a heart back and saved it. Then she slid into her starred album and whispered, "Hi, Mom," to a photo of Katherine Fletcher. She had this warm, big smile and framed her round belly with both hands. That was the day Lilith was born and Katherine died.

Lilith almost scrolled past. Then she stopped—a little boy stood in the background, clutching the same stuffed penguin Lilith had tucked under her head. Cold prickles ran up her arms. His face was half turned, slightly blurred, but the shape of his brows... the angle of his stare—it tugged at something uneasy inside her. The boy who had given her the purifier. *That couldn't be right. Could it?*

"That's impossible," she whispered, sliding her fingers across the screen to zoom in until the image went soft and blocky. Her phone refused to give her more detail, like it had hit a wall.

For a second, her pupils knifed into slits and her vision sharpened anyway. Not the screen. Her. The photo's edges snapped into focus and the boy's outline held for half a second. Then the pixels swam and he was gone from the picture. Only a smear remained, like a thumbprint dragged across the background.

A high-pitched shriek detonated inside her head. Lilith let the phone go and clapped her hands over her ears. The sound drilled straight through her palms, too sharp to be real, vibrating behind her eyes. "Aaargh," she choked out, curling into a ball until it finally subsided.

Her breath came fast, heart pounding. What was that? And who was that boy? Questions stampeded. No answers.

Knock, knock.

"Who is it?" Lilith called, massaging her temple and reaching for her phone before pushing herself upright.

"It's me, Jake. Ready to go?"

"Oh." Her stomach gave a weird little dip. *The library*. Right. "Yeah, just a sec."

She shoved the phone into her pocket like it might bite and grabbed her backpack before opening the door. "Hey."

Jake took one look at her and tilted his head. Even with his empathy blocker on, he still did that thing where he noticed too much. "You okay?"

"Yeah." Lilith waved it off, already stepping into the hallway before her brain could catch up. "Let's go."

He paused. "Actually, I brought this." He held out a book.

Mastering Powerful Beasts. It was the seventh creature book he'd given her that month. "Wait," she said, taking it. "Did you already go to the library without me? Betrayal." She pulled a playful pout and planted her hands on her hips.

"I had free time." He shrugged. "I marked the python chapter for you. This one shows the scale from different angles."

"Of course you did." Lilith flipped to the bookmark with a soft smile. "Thanks."

"What about Teams 101 practice instead of library then?" He grimaced. "Ring illusions are evil and the practical is coming up soon." He scratched his forehead. "I know Arthur's trapped in

Advanced Thunder Techniques, so we can't use our usual spot... but the Diplomatic Terrace should do until later today, right?"

"Sure," Lilith said a little too quickly. Getting her head busy with something else sounded good.

Jake huffed as they walked out of the Zeus Wing. "And who knows? Maybe we can finally figure out your second gift." He threw his hands up dramatically. "I've narrowed my suspect list to eight possible gods," he said, pulling a crumpled paper from his pocket.

Lilith raised an eyebrow. "Wasn't it six yesterday? This is called expanding, not narrowing."

Jake sighed like she was the one being unreasonable. "I realized I hadn't considered that your 'nature manipulation' might not be nature manipulation."

Lilith frowned. "Huh?"

"Like..." He slowed down. "What if you're not controlling nature?" He tapped the book against his palm. "What if you're messing with the rules around plants. Speeding up growth. Or making something look alive for a second when it's already dead. Like... an echo of what it used to be."

Lilith didn't know whether to laugh at the sheer extent of his theories or be impressed that the world still kept unfolding into new possibilities every day. "Well, if that's the case," she said, bumping his shoulder as they stepped onto the Diplomatic Terrace, "you can cross two of your new gods right back off."

She lifted an eyebrow, defiant. Her gaze snagged on a scrubby bush by the railing. The plant jerked like it had been yanked by invisible strings, then surged upward, splitting into branches until a small cherry tree stood where the bush had been. Leaves unfurled with a soft rush. Pale blossoms popped open, and for a second the air actually smelled sweeter. And it held in place.

Jake gaped. "Whoa. Since when can you do *that*?"

The terrace doors opened behind them. Adrien stepped out, wind tugging at his uniform collar. Hannah and Kami trailed after him, close enough to be together, far enough to look like they weren't. "Okay," Adrien said, eyes flicking from the cherry blossoms to Lilith's face. "What did I just walk into?"

"Just showing Jake I'm not a one-trick seed pony," Lilith said, grinning. "But we're about to practice illusions for the Ring Seekers challenge. You in?"

"Sure," Adrien said, smirking. "I'd love to beat you."

"Oh, hush." Lilith rolled her eyes, but she couldn't stop the half smile tugging at her mouth.

Jake clapped his hands. "Great. The more, the merrier. Let me see..." He snagged Lilith's bottle and twisted the cap.

"Hey, my bottle," Lilith protested.

"Borrowing it," Jake said as the tamper seal snapped. He flicked the thin plastic seal-ring free, screwed the cap back on, and handed the bottle to her. "There, you can have this back, and we have a ring." He held the seal up between two fingers.

Adrien smirked. "That's barely a ring."

"It fits." Jake shrugged. "Same rules: find it, wear it, win the challenge." He twirled his finger in the air. "I'll hide it. Now, turn around."

"I'll watch," Hannah said, drifting aside with Kami.

Adrien's smirk faltered. "Really? You're both just going to stand there?"

Hannah didn't answer. Kami's shoulders lifted in a small shrug that didn't reach her face.

Lilith leaned toward Adrien as they faced the wall. "Did I miss something?" she murmured.

Adrien exhaled through his nose, like he'd been holding it all day. "They're mad I went to the train wreck without them."

Lilith blinked. "Wait, the Ohio thing? That was forever ago!"

"Yeah, but..." Adrien dragged a hand through his hair. "Back then I told them we were assigned to collect mushrooms." His mouth tightened. "I didn't tell them I asked for the slip myself and left them out. They found out that part yesterday." His voice dropped. "In fact, they don't even know about the Atrium Roots either."

Lilith's expression softened. "Oh."

"So now I'm the villain," he muttered. "Which is impressive, considering I'm the one who got attacked. And the rogues were after the rest of my team, so technically I saved them." He made it sound cocky on purpose, like swagger was easier than admitting it stung.

"I'm sorry," Lilith said. "That whole mess... I'm sorry you got pulled into it."

"Nah." Adrien shook his head once. "That one's on me. I shouldn't have lied." He looked toward Hannah and Kami, then away. "They'll forgive me. Eventually." He tried a smile, but it didn't land. "New topic," he said, clearing his throat. "How have you been?"

"Fine, I guess. Just... working on the ritual stuff."

Adrien nodded. "Yeah. You're always buried in a book lately." He hesitated, then said it anyway. "I can't believe you're still going through with it."

Lilith shrugged. "How could I not? I don't know how Loopers do it. Spending their life collecting Life Powder from people... it feels like killing. Even when people say it isn't."

Adrien's breath left him slow. "I think the problem starts right there." His tone softened. "To me it's not killing. It's balance." He watched her like he was choosing the least-wrong words. "You haven't seen what it's like to give life yet. It's... different."

Lilith didn't answer. Her fingers tightened around the bottle.

"And if you think about it," Adrien added, "the end isn't really the end. Souls recycle. Some go to Elysium. Some come back to Earth..." He lifted a shoulder. "It's only sad if you hold it like a loss instead of a turning. Being a Looper is guiding people to the next part."

Lilith's brow furrowed. "Elysium... that's like heaven, right?"

Adrien nodded. "Sort of. There are a lot of places down there." He tilted his head. "But the point is, I don't see us as murderers. Life Powder is energy. It keeps the wheel moving."

Just then Jake popped between them. "Ready? Three, two, one, GO!"

"Beat me if you can, Feisty!" Adrien teased, dashing ahead.

"Hey, cheater!" Lilith yelled, bolting after him.

Adrien hovered his hands dramatically over the plants, like a fortune teller conjuring a vision, while Lilith pressed her cheek to the dirt, scanning for any trace of the ring. "Too easy!" he declared, holding the plastic ring up like a trophy.

What? Lilith didn't even see where it was hiding. She was still brushing soil off her face when Kallista strolled onto the terrace.

"I told you," Adrien bragged, "I'm crushing the ring practical next week. Nobody will beat me."

Kallista's lips curled as she came closer. "Cute. You remember the rules, right?"

"What are you talking about? I found it first," Adrien said.

Sweet as poison, Kallista hopped forward, plucked the ring from his fingers, and slid it onto her own. She offered him a taunting smile. "You can't win if you don't wear it. So, congrats... you just lost." She finished with a dramatic bow. Laughter burst from Hannah and the others.

Adrien scowled, folding his arms. "Very funny."

"It is funny because it's true," Kallista said. "The practical's full of decoys. Half the rings you find are bait, some are fakes, and some are traps." She waggled the ring on her finger. "You still have to identify the right one, and you still have to wear it."

Adrien rolled his eyes and waved a hand. "Whatever."

Kallista only smirked. "All right. Want me to hide it for you this time?"

"Please," Jake said, leaning back against the wall. "Can't wait to learn from the master."

Kallista made it look effortless. A flick of her fingers, a whisper of green, and one flower curled shut around the ring like it was protecting a secret.

This hunt lasted much longer than the first. The boy in the photo kept buzzing in the back of Lilith's skull, but she shoved the thought away and forced herself to focus on the ring. One impossible thing at a time. They searched until Adrien finally strode past, reached into the blooms, and plucked it out.

"Ugh, how?" Lilith groaned. "I literally can make flowers grow!"

The sun dipped lower, dragging shadows across the terrace. Adrien dusted a faint trail of Life Powder to catch on outlines and seams, but Lilith's Drakon-sight slid into place, scanning for the smallest betrayals of motion while using less energy.

At some point, Kami and Hannah changed their minds and joined the hunt. Soon, everyone was scouring the terrace garden, flipping leaves, checking tree hollows, even tapping statues for hidden compartments. Lilith bloomed every flower she could find, coaxing buds open with a stare for almost a full hour. Nothing.

"Got it!" Hannah declared this time, puffing out her chest.

"Finally," Kallista giggled. "Poor Jake needs an energy refill. He was making tiny portals and nudging the ring away every time someone got too close." She tossed her blue-flamed hair, laughing like she'd been waiting to spill it.

Jake groaned. "You weren't supposed to tell them that."

Kallista winked. "You deserve the credit." She paused and checked the time. "It's getting late. One last round?"

"Winning feels good. I'm in," Hannah said smugly.

"That was a one-time thing," Adrien grumbled. "Don't get used to it."

"Sure," Lilith said. Kami nodded too.

By then, the sky had gone dark enough that the terrace lanterns blinked awake one by one. Lilith checked the moonlit garden, then the ring, then the shadows under the railing. She didn't check the time. With only moonlight left to guide them, Adrien squinted, looking drained after handling Life Powder all afternoon. Kami conjured a small fire-orb that bobbed at her shoulder. Hannah stayed invisible, although Lilith didn't understand why. Maybe so she could snatch the ring from someone's hand before they put it on.

"Glad you're all having so much fun together." Arthur's voice came from the terrace entrance, flat as stone.

Lilith spun. Arthur stood in the doorway, arms crossed. His expression was unreadable, but his jaw was set, tight. Wrong.

Oh, no. They'd forgotten to message him. They were supposed to meet after he finished class, back when the sun was still up. Lilith's stomach dropped. She caught Jake's eye.

They'd messed up.

"We were just training for—" Jake started.

Arthur didn't wait to hear it. "Sure, Hills," he muttered, and walked past them toward the Zeus Wing. The group fell silent. Arthur's fists were clenched so tightly Lilith wondered if his knuckles might crack.

"What was that about?" Adrien asked, raising an eyebrow.

Lilith sighed, rubbing her face. "We forgot to tell him we were coming here. We were supposed to meet at the Phaunos Tree after his class."

Behind Adrien, a blue tulip blinked softly in the moonlight. There it was, tucked inside the petals.

Lilith reached around him and plucked the ring free. "I think it's time to call it a night," she said, slipping it onto her finger and forcing a smile.

"Yeah," Kallista agreed.

"Yep," Jake, Hannah, and Kami chorused.

"Fun killer," Adrien muttered under his breath.

"But hey," Kallista said, giving Lilith a nod. "You won this last one."

Lilith nodded back, but the victory felt hollow. Arthur's anger sat like a weight on her chest. And then moonlight snagged on something in Kallista's hair. Lilith's breath hitched and she tugged lightly on Jake's jacket as the group headed toward the wings. "Yeah?" he murmured.

"What are the chances?" she whispered. "Look at her hairpin."

Jake's gaze flicked up. His eyes widened. "No way." Tucked into Kallista's blue-flamed hair was a scale. Thin, iridescent, unmistakable. A python scale.

"Yes way," Lilith breathed, barely believing it herself.

"I could make a portal under the pin and..."

"I'm not a thief," Lilith cut in, sharper than she meant to. Jake groaned. "Then what?"

"I don't know." Lilith let out a slow breath. "We sleep on it. Tomorrow we'll figure something out."

Her voice softened. "Plus I need to talk to Arthur. We really dropped the ball."

"Are you two coming?" Adrien called when they lagged behind.

Lilith and Jake exchanged a glance, then jogged to catch up. They fell back into the group's easy chatter, but Lilith couldn't join in.

Her thoughts kept splitting in three directions: how to apologize to Arthur without making it worse, how to talk to Kallista to get that hairpin without dragging her into ritual insanity, and why that boy was in her mom's picture the day Lilith was born.

She had a long night ahead, and three problems that made falling asleep feel almost impossible.

CHAPTER TWENTY

CURSED HAMMER

L ilith couldn't sleep. Not with Arthur's face stuck in her head. She shoved the covers off, snatched her map, and wrote before she could chicken out.

> To: Arthur Owens
> *I'm sorry about today. Can we talk?*
> —L

Her waterbub sputtered before she could finish the rest of her signature, but the parchment drank the main message anyway.

That was what actually mattered. Arthur would know it was from her.

Lilith held the map in both hands and waited. Nothing. That was when the guilt really sank in. She knew that feeling: being left out. But this time it was different, she'd done it to someone else. Somehow, that felt worse. When sleep finally took her under, it didn't feel like resting. It felt like giving up.

A few hours later, Lilith woke up sweaty and tangled in her sheets, her heart punching hard like she'd sprinted across the Academy. The nightmare slid away the second she tried to grab it, leaving only scraps. A half-turned boy. A blur of a face. That awful wrongness in her head.

She rubbed her eyes and grabbed the map again. Still blank. Her stomach tightened right before a sharp flash lit the window. Not sunrise. Lightning.

Lilith stepped onto the balcony just in time to see a bolt rip the sky. The air smelled like wet stone and ozone. Her pupils tightened on instinct, and the grounds snapped into focus. The field near the treeline became crisp. Dark grass. Churned footprints. A lone figure moving between invisible targets. *Arthur.* He yanked another lightning from the sky and threw it again and again at Aegis targets he had created. It wasn't even five in the morning yet.

She swallowed. *Had he read her message and ignored it? Or had he missed it? Either way... how was she supposed to fix this?*

Lilith let out a long breath, went back inside, got dressed, and grabbed her map. It guided her through dim tunnels and quiet corridors. Two Acephali were already mopping, silent as ghosts. She slipped past them and kept going until the air turned cooler and greener and she stepped into one of the fields behind the Academy.

Arthur did not look like someone who wanted company. Lightning snapped so often the field strobed white, then gray, then white again. But she kept moving. When Lilith was about ten steps away, he yanked down another bolt and caught it in his hand. This time he didn't throw it. He just held it, blue-white and furious, the air around his knuckles sizzling. "What do you want?" he called, steady as a bell.

He didn't look at her. Didn't need to. Of course he knew she was there. His awareness was honestly unfair.

"On a scale of one to ten," she called, "how mad are you? Eleven?"

Arthur squeezed the bolt between his hands until it was gone, but he still didn't turn around. "Why would I be mad, Fletcher?"

"Well..." Lilith slowed, boots damp in the grass. "If I were you, I'd be upset. And last night you seemed..."

"My usual self," he cut in, voice flat.

Lilith crossed her arms. "Okay. Now you definitely sound mad."

A bolt cracked overhead but Arthur didn't flinch. He exhaled hard through his nose and finally looked at her. Not angry, exactly. Just tight. She could really use Jake right now to translate him into something understandable.

Lilith's throat bobbed. She forced herself to meet his eyes anyway. "I wanted to apologize," she said, and hated that it almost came out like a question.

Arthur's mouth twitched like he wanted to laugh and couldn't. "Why bother?"

"Because I messed up and we're a team," Lilith said. The words came out steadier than she felt.

He gave a short scoff. "You only care about ditching this place. So no, we aren't."

It stung, quick and sharp. "Maybe I don't plan on staying forever," she said, "but that doesn't change the fact that we're friends. Team or not."

Arthur went very still. "...Did you just call me your friend?"

Lilith blinked, thrown by the shift in his voice. "I mean... aren't you?"

For a split second it seemed like he was startled by the idea and didn't know what to do with it. Then he shoved it away so fast it was almost impressive. "Never mind," he muttered, looking past her again. "We're good."

Lilith eyed him. "Really? Just like that?"

"Yes," he said, and interlaced his fingers, the way he did when he quizzed her and she finally got the answer right.

Lilith wasn't sure she believed him. She also wasn't sure how they'd gone from almost-a-friendship-disaster to "we're good" in under a minute. But she wasn't about to question it. "If it makes you feel any better, I got stomped like a bug in that practice."

Arthur's mouth tilted into the smallest smirk. "I know."

Lilith rolled her eyes. "Wow. Thanks. Super encouraging."

He shrugged, like truth was a hobby. "It is what it is."

"Okay," Lilith said, pointing at the sky. "Since you clearly know everything, how about showing me some tricks?"

"...Sure," he said slowly.

"Cool." She nodded, patting her pockets. "But first I need to send Jake a note. I'm not pulling the 'forgetting people' thing twice in one week." Then she groaned. "Oh, perfect. I forgot to refill it." She glared at her waterbub like it had betrayed her personally. "Do you have one with you?"

Arthur's eyes lingered on her map, like he could still see the message that had flashed there hours ago. His mouth twitched in a way Lilith had never seen before. "So... L," he said, drawing out the only letter she'd managed to sign before her waterbub sputtered dry the night before.

Lilith blinked. Not because it proved he'd read her message, but because Arthur didn't do this. He didn't even use first names. He *definitely* didn't use nicknames.

He cleared his throat, but the almost-smile didn't fully leave. "You've got to catch up on your spells," he said. "You've been here too long to rely only on a map and a phone." He pushed his sleeve up.

Lilith's gaze snagged on the ink-dark lightning bolt on his forearm. She'd never dared to ask why it was already permanent. None of their classmates had marks like that. Arthur looked up, as if listening for time itself, then dragged his fingers across the bolt. Golden letters ignited, spinning and stitching together until they folded into a tiny bird of light. It fluttered once and streaked toward the Academy.

Her mouth fell open and Arthur reached out and tapped her chin, nudging it shut with a smug little smirk. "There. Breathe."

"What was that?" she whispered.

"A message spell," Arthur said, casual like he hadn't just made her brain short-circuit. "No waterbub needed. The words find the recipient and show up on a nearby surface. But the farther it has to go, or the longer the message, the harder it is to hold."

"That's..." Lilith stared after the fading glow, looking for a word that fit. "That's amazing."

"Come on. I'll teach you." He bumped her shoulder like it was nothing.

And then he did. Over the next few days, Arthur didn't just show her one spell. He showed her shortcuts. Fixes. Little tricks that made magic behave the way it was supposed to. Between training, Jake's relentless attempts to sharpen his empathy skills, the looming Ring Seekers challenge, and Lilith's ritual plans, she somehow ended up spending more time with the two of them than she ever expected. Things were back to normal. Which, in her life, usually meant *enjoy it while it lasts.*

With about a month left before the Minotaur lesson, they still hadn't found a clean way to get a python scale. Nothing that didn't involve Kallista's hairpin. Still, they kept trying. A late-night research session here, a peek into the greenhouse supply closet there, until Jake came up with a new idea.

"Meet me at the open field around eleven," he had told them at breakfast before class. Genius or chaos, it was always hard to tell with Jake. Either way, it was usually worth showing up. Lilith arrived there too early and lingered while waiting. She lifted her purifier, watching it catch the sun. Light fractured into bright seams, as if the air itself had been stitched with shimmer. She flexed her fingers and coaxed a thin thread of Life Powder into the open.

Still unreal that something so small could tip the world between life and death.

"WATCH OUT!" The shout ripped through the quiet behind her. Lilith startled so hard the thread snapped, gold flecks scattering off her fingers as something huge tore through the air with a savage *whoosh*.

She hit the ground without thinking.

A hammer whipped past where her head had been, spinning like it had been thrown by someone showing off in an Ares drill. Christopher Fox's kind of move. Except the field was empty.

"What..." Lilith gasped, scrambling up. "Ruby! What's going on?"

"It's my forge project!" Ruby shouted without slowing. "It was supposed to return when called, not attack people!" Her face was tight with panic. "It went insane! I have to catch it. It can't leave Academy grounds!"

Lilith chased after her in time to see the hammer slam into a tree with a splintering crack. Shards of wood burst outward before it tore free and shot off again.

Ruby flung a fireball. It veered, clipped another trunk, and flames licked up the bark before sputtering out.

"You'll burn the whole forest down!" Lilith shouted, forcing her fear down hard. "We can't outrun this..." Her pupils tightened. Drakon-sight slid into place. The hammer's wild spin stopped being chaos and started being pattern. A stutter in its arc. A bias in its pull, like something kept yanking it forward. "But we can slow it down!"

Lilith teleported toward the edge of the Academy's boundary. The protective dome shimmered faintly if you caught it at the right angle, like heat over stone. *Please work.* She yanked Life Powder from her purifier and built a wall in the hammer's path.

The hammerhead struck without mercy, shattering the barrier like brittle glass. Lilith didn't stop. She built a second. A third. The hammer hit, slowed for half a heartbeat, then punched through. *It was working!*

A fourth barrier cracked, groaning under the impact.

"It won't stop!" Ruby's voice pitched sharp, panic fraying into desperation.

"It will!" Lilith's pulse roared in her ears. Her purifier was running on fumes. She snapped the scattered Powder back to herself like reeling in string, packed it tight, and put up two more walls. Not as much as before. But thicker. Heavier.

The hammer hit the first new barrier and this time it stuck, wedged deep enough that the whole thing shuddered. It fought to free itself like a trapped animal.

Ruby skidded in, breath ragged. "For a second, I thought you'd be flattened," she gasped. "I've never seen a hammer act like that, it—"

"Ruby!" Lilith snapped. Sweat slid down her neck. Her arms shook as the barrier trembled again.

"Sorry." Ruby lunged for the handle. Her fingers grazed it, but the hammer jerked and slipped away. "Come on," she hissed, trying again.

A bolt of lightning split the sky. Arthur dropped into view in a crackle of blue-white. "Need a hand?" he called, right as the hammer slammed into Lilith's last barrier with a brutal, bone-rattling impact.

The shock punched through her chest and sent her skidding backward, over the shimmer line and outside the Academy's protective spell, but she didn't let her powder barrier dissipate. Sucking in a sharp breath, she steadied her voice. "Arthur, shield it. Ruby, melt it!"

"On it." Arthur stepped in, just outside the boundary, and thrust his hands forward.

His Aegis snapped around the hammer in a tight sphere. Ruby thrust both hands toward it right before the shield sealed, her Hephaestus mark flaring.

Heat roared up, bright enough to bleach the air. The hammer shrieked. Something thin and furious, like a living thing trapped and screaming. Then it gave way, fracturing and collapsing into a writhing pool of black liquid, contained inside the Aegis.

Arthur's expression darkened. "It's cursed. Bennett, purify it!"

Ruby's eyes widened before she clenched her fists. Flames surged into a searing white as they swallowed the sludge. The shriek sharpened into a razor-edged wail that sliced straight through Lilith's skull. All three clapped their hands over their ears. And then... nothing.

Silence hit so hard Lilith's knees buckled. She dropped onto the dirt, breathing in broken pulls. "I'm okay," she managed, blinking up at them like the ground had tilted.

Ruby, still shaking, held her hand over the cooling remains. With a small flick of her fingers, the metal swirled, compressed, and reshaped into a solid orb. It pulsed once, then dulled as it settled into the grass.

Lilith pushed herself upright. "Whew. Can someone—"

"What's that?" Ruby cut in, staring past Lilith's shoulder.

Arthur's face went cold. "Fletcher, move!"

Lilith didn't have time. Lightning snapped down twice, and Arthur threw his Aegis over her at the last second. The first bolt slammed into the shield and skittered across it in a blinding sheet of light. For one breath, Lilith thought it had worked. The second bolt tore sideways before anyone could react and struck Ruby in the chest. She flew backward and hit the ground just inside the Academy's boundary, motionless.

Arthur glanced over his shoulder, eyes widening for half a second, as if he couldn't understand how someone had gotten hurt on his watch.

"Ruby!" Lilith's voice cracked.

A laugh rolled from above. A woman's laugh, muffled by cloud and distance, but heavy with threat. Another bolt arced for Arthur. He let go of the shield over Lilith and twisted, deflecting the strike with a sharp snap of light.

"I only want her," snarled the rogue woman hovering in the stormlit sky. "Just go."

Nausea crashed over Lilith. A drilling whine rose in her skull, louder and sharper with every breath. Not the cursed hammer's shriek. This was the same wrong note from the car accident and the photo on her phone. Her vision pinched tight. Her teeth clenched. *Breathe. Just breathe.*

Arthur straightened, lightning crackling between his fingertips as he stepped in front of Ruby like he could block the sky itself.

"You are not taking anyone," he said, voice ice-cold.

The rogue hurled a bolt straight at him. Arthur caught it midair, twisted the energy in his grip, and threw it back.

That was Lilith's opening.

I'm coming, Ruby.

Lilith lunged, one hand hooking Ruby's limp arm inside the shimmer line, the other catching Arthur's ankle on the far side. Her wrist mark ignited, heat flooding her veins. Light snapped blue and the world folded. Her legs trembled, refusing to hold her weight a second longer and her vision blurred into a creeping, absolute black as she hit the floor.

When Lilith came to, a bitter taste coated her tongue. A gentle warmth spread through her limbs, chasing away the heavy fog in her mind. She blinked against the soft glow of enchanted wards.

The infirmary. Shelves lined with teas, roots, herbs, and potions. A quiet hum in the air. Ruby lay on the other side of the room, too still, too pale.

Arthur stood beside Lilith with a small cup in his hand. "Will she be all right?" he asked, glancing toward Ruby.

Professor Thomas, hunched over a tray, nodded. "Yes, yes. Miss Bennett will need a few days, but she'll recover." Her eyes shifted to Lilith. "And you, Miss Fletcher. Did the serum help? How are you feeling?"

Lilith tried to sit up, her head still swimming. "Yeah... I think so. I'm okay."

Arthur offered the cup again. "You should drink more."

Lilith wrinkled her nose. "No, thanks." Whatever that was, it worked, but she was not doing that twice.

Professor Thomas moved to Ruby's side, layered gauze over a wound on her leg, then dripped an oozy potion onto it. Her mark glowed as she conjured a spirit arrow and sent it gently into Ruby's chest. Ruby let out a faint groan, but didn't wake.

"She'll be fine," Professor Thomas said, already turning toward the door. "I need to check with Principal Stewart about additional wards. You two rest."

Then she was gone. Lilith exhaled slowly and finally looked at Arthur. "How long was I out? And... does everyone know what happened?" Her voice wavered. "Is everyone okay?"

"About fifteen minutes," Arthur said, arms crossing. "And yes. I told them a rogue attacked and that the hammer was cursed. Everyone else is fine."

"So that woman was a rogue," Lilith said, swallowing. "I always pictured rogues as... I don't know. Black cloaks. Red eyes. But she looked normal. How did she even get so close to the Academy? I thought rogues didn't take risks like that."

"Slow down, Fletcher." Arthur's tone stayed clipped, but softer than usual. "Yes, a rogue. Gifted by Hera, from what I could tell. And you're right—most rogues avoid the Academy." His expression darkened. "And it's even stranger that she was alone. We don't hear of lone rogues often."

Lilith's throat tightened. "I don't even know how you found me and Ruby back there, but I'm glad you did."

Arthur's mouth twitched. "Fireballs exploding in the forest are hard to miss." He looked away. "I arrived early to meet you and Jake and saw trouble."

"Oh," Lilith blurted. "Jake! We were supposed to meet him!"

"It's fine," Arthur said. "I already sent him a message."

Relief slipped out of her in a shaky breath. "Thanks." Lilith's eyes flicked to Ruby again, and her stomach sank. "Why would a rogue go after Ruby?"

Arthur held her eyes for a long beat. "She didn't want Ruby," he said slowly. "She wanted you."

CHAPTER TWENTY-ONE

DOWN MEMORY LANE

The next morning, Lilith moved through the Academy's quiet halls, her footsteps swallowed by thick stone. The lingering scent of healing herbs clung to her clothes, a reminder of her restless night in the infirmary. Arthur and Jake were waiting for her in the small library. No teasing.

Without a word, they slipped past the shelves and down into the hidden space below. Lilith dropped onto a cold stone bench and exhaled. Her fingers traced mindless lines over the rock, as if she could scratch out an answer.

"Why me?" The words came out small, but they landed heavy.

She looked from Jake to Arthur, waiting for one of them to say, *Oh, it's obviously this*. Waiting for a reason that made any kind of sense.

Jake rubbed his temples. "Okay," he said, like he was resetting his brain. "Let's replay it. Cursed hammer goes feral. That was bait." He looked up, eyes sharp behind his glasses. "Then the rogue drops in and starts throwing lightning like it's confetti. Ruby gets hit, but she wasn't the target." He stared at Lilith. "You were."

Arthur's jaw flexed. He didn't argue. He didn't soften it, either. He only nodded, standing there tight as a locked door.

Silence filled the vault again.

Lilith swallowed. "What if…" She stopped, because saying it out loud felt like inviting it to be true.

"What?" Jake asked. His usual playfulness was gone.

Lilith glanced between them. "What if it ties back to the boy who gave me my purifier?" A faint, shrill hum prickled at the edge of her hearing. *Not again*. She winced and pressed her fingers to her temple.

Arthur's eyes narrowed. "You all right?"

"It's happening again," she said, forcing the words out. "That awful ringing." She swallowed. "It happened when that woman showed up yesterday, just like it did the night of my birthday. And the day I found the photo of the boy on my phone." Her voice wavered. "Or maybe it was my imagination. Maybe I'm losing it."

Arthur and Jake exchanged a quick, wary look.

Lilith's frustration flared. "What are you not saying?" She knew them well enough by now to recognize when their gears were turning.

"That…" Arthur said slowly, "sounds less like imagination and more like an erased memory trying to claw its way back."

Lilith shot to her feet. "Erased memory? Why in the world would anyone erase my memory?" Her voice climbed with disbelief. "That makes no sense."

Jake hesitated, worrying the edge of his sleeve between his fingers. "I was thinking the same thing."

Arthur's tone stayed practical. "There's always a reason to erase a memory." He nodded toward Jake. "But if that is the case, we have one option worth trying to test the theory."

Lilith turned, still trying to catch up. "Huh?"

"Apollo's apprentices can do more than visions and prophecies…" Arthur said. "They can read memories."

Jake's shoulders twitched. Was Arthur suggesting what she thought he was?

"No way. I've studied the technique," Jake said quickly, the words tumbling over each other. A thread of panic slipped into his voice. "But I've never actually done it. I mean, gathering geographic intel from owls doesn't count as real experience."

Lilith's stomach tightened. "Are we talking about looking inside my head? Like the Oracle?"

"Kind of. *Technically.*" Jake winced. "But I've never done it on a real person before. Maybe, and I mean really maybe, I could try—if you wanted me to. But I doubt I'd pick up anything useful. I can't break walls. I only know the basics."

"You can do it, Hills," Arthur said, like he was announcing the weather.

Jake swallowed. Pride and fear wrestled across his face. "I can…try," he said, quieter now. "If Lilith wants me to."

"I'll tell you what," Arthur said. "Test run. Read mine first."

Jake blinked, then nodded a little too fast. "Okay. One memory. Just the rogue attack."

"Perfect," Arthur said. Calm. Unmoving. "I'll even hold back, so you'll have to work for it."

Lilith hovered a step closer. "And I just stand here?"

"Yes," Arthur said without looking at her. "Just observe."

Jake stretched his fingers before pressing the inside of his wrist to Arthur's forehead, right between his brows. At first, nothing happened. Then both boys went still. Not statue-still. More like someone had unplugged them. Their eyes turned cloudy and pale, the color draining until they looked like frosted glass.

"What's happening?" Lilith whispered.

The air in the vault tightened, stretched thin. Lilith leaned in, trying to see their faces, when a hard, invisible shove slammed into her chest and tossed her backward. She stumbled into a stone bench. At the same time, Jake and Arthur were flung apart like a cord had snapped. Jake hit one wall with a grunt. Arthur slammed into the other and sprang upright instantly, lightning flickering at his fingertips.

Arthur's eyes flashed. "What do you think you're doing?"

Jake flinched, hands flying up. "I'm sorry. I didn't mean to. I lost control."

Lilith rushed between them. "Whoa!"

Arthur's jaw flexed. The lightning dimmed, but his posture stayed locked. "That's off-limits," he snapped.

"I'm sorry!" Jake's voice cracked. He pushed his glasses up with a shaking finger. "Your mind had locks everywhere. I didn't know where to go. I didn't mean to see that. I told you I had never done it before!"

Arthur stared at him for a beat, breathing slowly through his nose. Then he looked at Lilith. "Enough practice," he said, his voice still sharp but more controlled. His gaze shifted to Lilith. "If you still want answers, he can try yours."

Jake swallowed again. "Did you not see what happened just now?"

Arthur didn't hesitate. "Yes, I was there." His mouth tightened. "You were making your way inside my head, which means you can read hers." He tipped his head toward Lilith. "And right now, Hills, you're the safest option we have."

Lilith blinked. "Err..."

"Fletcher, if your memories are glitching, he's your best bet," Arthur said. "Not because he's an expert. Because he knows enough, and because no one else has to find out what we've been doing this year." His gaze shifted to Jake. "Are you up for this, Hills?"

Jake's face flickered with something suspiciously like pride. "I can't promise much, but I can give it a try if you want me to."

Even though her stomach was turning, Lilith knew Jake had her back. "I trust you."

Jake drew a long breath and took a careful step closer. "Okay. Look at me," he said softly. "If anything feels wrong, you say stop. Okay?"

Arthur's voice cut in, steady and sharp. "And I'll interfere if things go south."

Jake nodded. "Understood."

Lilith stepped closer to Jake, palms damp. "Okay. What do I do?"

"Lower your defenses," Jake said, gentler now.

"How?" She winced. "I mean, are they even up?"

"It's human nature," Jake said. "Just hold on to one thing. The moment it started. The hammer. The rogue. The sound. Try not to think about anything else."

Lilith nodded, focusing on his eyes behind the square frames. *Hammer. Ruby. The sky splitting open.*

Jake raised his wrist toward her forehead. His eyes turned opaque and bright, like tunnels opening behind the glassy surface. Then the vault fell away, like she was slipping underwater.

Images snapped into place, one after another, like pages flipping. A hammer spinning through sunlight. Ruby sprinting, panic stamped across her face. Fire bursting wild and crooked. Life Powder flaring gold. Walls rising. Shattering. Arthur dropping in, lightning crackling in his hands. The rogue woman in the clouds, smiling like she owned the sky.

Then... *blank.*

But there was something inside—a hole. A missing page. Lilith reached for it, but her fingers passed through it like smoke. A flash swallowed everything. And the rogue woman appeared again, younger this time. Somewhere in her teens, maybe, but still recognizable. The same sharp features. The same dangerous confidence, only not fully grown into itself yet.

Another flash.

This time, it was Lilith's old house. Maybe the one they'd lived in when she was around six, back in Salt Lake City. She wasn't sure. It had been so long ago... Then there was more. The living room. The couch—it smelled like lemon. Because little Lilith had spilled a carton of chocolate milk and someone had helped her clean it up with lemon-scented spray. For one flickering second, Lilith thought it was her dad. But no. It was a boy. His face flashed. That brow. That dark hair. Lilith's breath caught. It was him. The boy from the accident, only younger.

Her chest tightened so hard it hurt. It was like watching a movie of her own life and realizing whole scenes had been stolen from her. *Did someone really erase my mind?* She strained toward the memory, craving to see more.

Another flash. A second boy, older, stood behind them. Lilith didn't recognize that one. She tried to focus, tried to make the memory sharpen, but he was half hidden in the doorway.

Then... *blank.* And a voice echoing in the walls of her head. "Goodbye, sis." *Flash.* Standing by the front door was the first boy again. He stepped closer and kissed little Lilith on the forehead. She could feel the warmth. She wanted to shout. To ask who he was. But she was trapped inside a younger version of herself, inside a memory she could not change. The boy patted her head, and something glowed around his wrist—a purifier. *Maybe the same one he had given her.*

Lilith's stomach dropped as he stepped backward and touched the shoulders of the two teens behind him—the older boy and the girl from the stormlit sky. Light flared blue and the three of them vanished.

Blank.

Blank.

Blank.

Pressure built inside Lilith's ribs, squeezing her chest from the inside.

"Jake," Arthur's voice said, muffled, like it was coming through stone. "Bring her back."

Lilith gasped. She was on her knees, back in the vault. Tears poured down her face, though she didn't know when they had started. Her breath hitched, her lungs fighting to pull in enough air.

Jake stumbled backward like he'd been punched. Arthur grabbed him by the shoulders. Not rough, but firm. Grounding. "Breathe, Hills." Then he looked over his shoulder. "Fletcher, you all right?"

Jake swallowed hard, eyes wide. "I—I..."

Lilith wiped her face with the back of her hand, blinking through the blur. "I'm okay."

Arthur didn't seem to believe her. He moved closer and lowered himself to her eye level, like he knew she needed someone right there in case she broke apart. Lilith lowered herself onto the floor, Arthur's hand settled on her shoulder, steadying her. She didn't startle. She hadn't even registered him crossing the space between them. Then he glanced at Jake. "Did you find anything?"

Jake looked at Arthur, then at Lilith, like he hated every word he had to say. "It was an erased memory," he said. "Really buried." His voice dropped to a whisper. "Lilith had a brother."

The words hit her harder than the invisible shove had.

Jake continued slowly. "A Looper. The same boy who died in the car accident."

Lilith shook her head, fast and desperate. "It must be a mistake. That's not possible. Is it?"

Jake's voice cracked. "I'm sorry, Lilith." He swallowed. "And that rogue woman from the attack," he added, quieter, "she wasn't random. She knew your brother. She was with him before your memory was erased."

Silence slammed down on the vault. Lilith's hands trembled. "Why was she after me?"

Arthur's gaze sharpened, dangerous and focused. "Maybe because whatever they erased," he said slowly, "she's afraid it didn't stay erased." He paused, his thumb brushing absently over the scar on his lip. "Or maybe because your brother joined the rogues, and they always need to wipe their old lives away before they can vanish."

"I never should've tried to do this." Jake's voice was wrecked. "I'm so sorry, Lilith. I shouldn't have gone that deep. I didn't—"

Lilith shook her head. "I asked you to," she said, her voice hoarse. "I *had* to know. I just don't understand." Her throat tightened. "Why?"

Arthur's tone turned quiet and careful. "Cutting ties is part of the process. No family. No friends. Nothing left behind." His voice lowered. "Rogues can't vanish if there are people connected to them, looking for them."

Lilith's stomach twisted. "But why would he choose to become a rogue?" Her voice came out sharper than she meant it to. "Be a bad guy?"

"We don't know the whole story," Jake said gently. "But at the end, your brother protected you, right? That has to mean something."

Lilith wiped fresh tears away. "I don't even know his name."

Jake hesitated before murmuring, "Nathan Zeke Fletcher."

Nathan. The name felt both foreign and familiar, like a song she hadn't heard in years but somehow still knew all the words to.

Arthur's steady gaze locked onto hers as he squeezed her shoulder lightly. "Are you okay?"

Lilith looked at him. Really looked. The sharpness in his features had softened, like he wanted to understand what she was feeling instead of just observing it from a distance. "I..." She wiped her face again. "I think so." Then she remembered the way Arthur had reacted when Jake had tried to read him. "Is that what happened to you earlier, too? When Jake tried to read you?" she asked quietly.

Arthur exhaled. "Not really," he said. "Hills got too close to memories of my father. Memories I barely remembered myself." He glanced at Jake. "I lost my temper." Jake looked down. Arthur ran a hand through his hair.

"I'll never understand why your father is so..." She rubbed her nose, still trying to settle her breathing. "I don't even know how to say it. Why does he treat you like that?"

Arthur's jaw tensed. For a moment, he said nothing. Then finally, in a quiet voice, he said, "Because he thinks I deserve it."

Lilith stared at him. Her grief shifted sideways for one second, making room for something hot and indignant. "Wait," she said. "You know he's wrong, right?" Arthur didn't answer. "Nobody deserves to be treated like that," she said, more forcefully than she intended. "Especially not you."

Something flickered in Arthur's emerald eyes. Something new Lilith couldn't name. It was like she had unlocked a door he'd kept tightly shut. He looked like he wanted to say something else, but instead, he only nodded once and silence stretched between them. Not uncomfortable. Not tense. Just there.

Jake sighed. "If we ever do this craziness again," he muttered, "I'm wearing three hundred empathy blockers. Maybe then I won't cry like a baby."

Lilith let out a small, wet laugh. "Deal."

"If?" Arthur raised an eyebrow.

Lilith looked between them. Jake, pale but still trying to make her laugh. Arthur, guarded and bruised in places he rarely let anyone see, still close enough to keep her steady.

Not in her wildest dreams would she have guessed she had a brother. Let alone that she would never see him again. That he was gone. The truth still hurt, and most of it was still buried somewhere she couldn't reach. But she knew one thing—*if she had to fall apart, she would have chosen this exact room. These exact two people.*

But she didn't break into pieces. Not completely. Because somehow, Arthur and Jake didn't let her carry it all alone.

Chapter Twenty-Two

A MYSTERIOUS DELIVERY

Lilith's head was still spinning, even days after learning the truth: Nathan, the boy who had awakened her gift, was her brother. *Her brother.*

The thought still felt foreign. Yet random memories of him kept surfacing in her sleep, uninvited and unclear. *Were they real, or just her mind playing tricks on her?*

"Goodbye, sis!" Nathan stood in the doorway of their old house, waving with that crooked grin. "I love you." Then suddenly—she was in the middle of the street, the evening of her birthday. The headlights. The crash. "Nooo!" Lilith jerked awake—only to roll straight off her bed. "Ow," she groaned, slamming against the floor.

She rubbed her arm and stayed there, too tired to move.

The dream clung to her like mist—fading but still lingering, refusing to fully disappear. It was often the same: Nathan hugging her, promising to always watch over her. *So why had he left? Why had her brother become a rogue? Was she ever going to really find the answers she had been looking for?*

No matter how many times Jake tried, the visions stayed blurry. They weren't as painful anymore, but they were still fragmented. *Still missing too much.* She needed a Mnemosyne apprentice. Someone who actually knew how to untangle memories and weave through someone's mind without making a mess of it. But she couldn't risk letting a stranger know about the vault. About the ritual.

Her alarm shrieked, and she sighed. *Morning already?* Even exhausted, she got ready. One step at a time. She'd barely finished fixing her tie when her phone buzzed.

"Lilly! Guess what?! I did a cartwheel—ON PURPOSE!" Amy's excited voice burst through the speaker, energy so infectious that Lilith couldn't help but laugh—she even snorted. She needed that dose of Amy. It should have been prescribed to her.

"Hey, troublemaker. Are you talking to your sister?" Nicholas's voice came next, and Amy giggled. "Hey, bud," he said, popping his head into view. "How's school treating you?"

Lilith's brows lifted slightly. Her dad checking in—actually caring—still felt strange. But kind of nice.

Meghan appeared behind Amy, gently pulling her curls into a ponytail. "You look tired, sweetheart," she signed, concerned. "Long night?"

"Yeah," Lilith signed back, moving her fist up and down.

It wasn't hard to steer the conversation toward lighter things: Amy's latest swimming lesson, Nicholas's patient stories, and Meghan's busy workday. When the call ended, Lilith tucked her phone into her jacket and double-checked that she had everything she needed for the Ring Seekers challenge.

"Aaaah!" She tripped on her way out of the room, barely catching herself against the doorframe. "Is gravity mad at me, or is it kiss-the-floor day?" she muttered, checking her knees, but her eyes landed on something else—a small brown package by her feet.

Lilith frowned. Packages passed through wards, checks, and at least three adults who loved making things complicated before being delivered. Except this one had no stamps, no sender.

The wrapping was rough, like butcher paper tied with twine. Scribbled across the front in shaky handwriting were three letters:

> *L. A. F.*

Was it from another student? Or a teacher? Lilith stared at it as if it could bite.

First, she sniffed it; then she shook it. "All right, let's see..." she mumbled, carefully untying the string. The paper fell away, revealing an unfamiliar jeweled bracelet. Her body tensed. She crumpled the paper around it and stuffed it into her jacket—if there was one thing she had learned this year, it was never—ever—touch an unknown artifact with bare hands.

Where were Arthur, Jake, or Adrien when she needed them? *What would they say? Arthur would probably be all logic and caution, telling her not to trust. Adrien? He'd grin, call it a gift from the gods, and dare her to test it.* Lilith exhaled, shaking her head. *Jake? He would—*

Whoosh.

Lilith froze halfway down the Diplomatic Terrace, whipping around. Only to spot a few birds in the courtyard and Professor Goldsmith chatting with apprentices in the corner. But something still felt off. Her skin prickled, and she quickened her pace. *Whoosh*—her breath hitched. She turned around—still nothing. The uneasy feeling crawled up her spine.

"FLIPPING TOOTHPICKS!" Lilith nearly jumped out of her own skin when she turned back to keep heading toward the dining hall and Jake was right there. Had he materialized?

Jake hopped back, looking just as startled. "S-sorry?" he stammered. "I didn't mean to scare you."

Lilith pressed a hand to her racing heart. "I thought someone was—never mind. I need to talk to you!"

Jake blinked, adjusting his glasses. "Uh... okay?" He glanced around. "Are we dodging assassins or something?"

Lilith rolled her eyes and grabbed his arm, dragging him into the nearest empty room.

"What's with the secrecy?" he joked. "Oh, WAIT! Did you get the python scale?" His eyes lit up.

"No, no." Lilith shook her head, pulling the small brown package from her jacket. "I gotta ask you something. This—do you know what it is? Did you leave it by my door?"

"Huh?" Jake's curiosity turned to pure shock. His jaw dropped. "Oh! Wowie, wowie, wowzers!" He took the paper-wrapped bracelet carefully, holding it by the edges.

Lilith folded her arms, unimpressed. "I'm gonna take that as a 'yes' for the first question and 'no' to the second."

Jake wasn't listening. His eyes gleamed like he'd just discovered a lost treasure.

"This can't be real," he muttered under his breath. "If it is what I think it is—"

"Earth to Jake." Lilith snapped her fingers.

Jake finally looked up. "Who gave this to you?"

"If I knew, I wouldn't have asked if you left it by my door," she replied, tapping her foot.

"You can't blame me for getting distracted," he said with a shrug. "Maybe it was Arthur?"

She shook her head. "Arthur would've given it to me in person."

"I guess you're right. Maybe Adrien?"

"C'mon, he'd make a whole event out of it. Probably with fireworks."

Jake muffled a giggle and scratched his chin. "Then I have no clue. But I think this is the Hypnos Inhibitor? Unless it's a prank. It's a prank, right?"

"No pranks. Not from me, at least. Wait, the what now?" Lilith asked.

Jake grinned. "A relic created for one of Zeus's mortal favorites to protect her from Hera's mind control. Legend says whoever wears it can't be manipulated—though illusions would still fool you."

Lilith frowned. "You're saying it blocks mind control?"

"Basically. But I've only seen paintings of it in the archives." Jake used the paper to flip the bracelet over, inspecting every groove, clasp, and tiny engraved symbol. His excitement dimmed into concentration.

Lilith watched him for a few seconds. "Should I be worried that you suddenly look like Principal Stewart during my skills assessment?"

"Shh. Curse check." Jake held the bracelet closer to the light, then traced a careful circle over it with one finger.

His mark glowed, and a faint gold shimmer crawled over the metal and vanished.

He did it again, slower this time. Then a third time, muttering under his breath.

Lilith raised an eyebrow. "How many curse checks do you know?"

"After the hammer tried to turn you guys into pancakes? All of them." He glanced up. "Or, well, all I could find in the library without needing a restricted pass." He studied the bracelet again. "No binding curse. No possession residue. No blood lock. No sleeper hex. No obvious trap spell."

"That's... comforting?" Lilith said.

"It's not a guarantee," Jake admitted, handing it back carefully. "Ancient relics can hide things regular tests miss. But if this is a prank, it's very expensive and probably curse-free." His gaze dropped to the bracelet. "And if it really is the Hypnos Inhibitor, the protection could be huge. Wearing it today might not be the worst idea."

"I'm sorry, what?" Lilith's eye twitched. "I don't just put on random enchanted objects."

Jake snorted. "Really?" His gaze dropped pointedly to her pendant.

Lilith rolled her eyes. "Not since I found out magic is real, at least," she said, crossing her arms the same way Amy did whenever she begged Meghan for extra dessert, frown and pursed lips included. Then she sighed and reached for the bracelet.

Mind control. Erased memories. A rogue who knew her brother. If this thing was real, it might be a risk worth taking.

"Fine," she said. "But if my eyes glow red or I start speaking ancient owl, I'm blaming you." Lilith snapped the bracelet onto her wrist.

A pulse of golden light shot out, wrapping around her like a cocoon.

The magic rippled through her body, warm and weightless. For a moment, it felt like she was standing in a dream—then, just as fast, it vanished.

Lilith blinked. "That's it?"

"Huh. That was... anticlimactic." Jake shrugged.

"Are we sure this isn't just fancy jewelry?" She lifted her wrist, tilting it.

"Could be. Or not. But if you're going to test it, today's probably the safest day to do it. Lots of eyes, teachers..."

Lilith stared at him. "During Ring Seekers?"

"It's not an official skill-level check," Jake said. "It's a challenge, so defensive relics are allowed." He nodded toward her sleeve. "And hide it. You don't have to announce what relics you're carrying. I've seen Adrien carrying at least three different ones during challenges. His family has dozens."

"Okay, I won't take it off just yet," Lilith said, tugging her sleeve down. "We should go. The challenge starts soon, and I haven't had breakfast."

"All right, let's grab something quick. I'm starving," he said, heading to the door.

They joined the throngs of apprentices crowding the corridors, Jake rambling on about more deity tools than Lilith could keep up with. By the time they reached the dining hall, the rush had thinned.

Jake paused near the entrance. "Gonna grab oatmeal. Meet you at the table?"

Lilith nodded. "Sure, I'll save you a seat over there," she said, pointing at one of the tables to their left.

After filling her plate with an omelet and a muffin, Lilith took out her map and scrawled a quick note to Arthur:

> *There was a mysterious bracelet by my door today. Jake says it blocks mind control. Ever heard of it?*
> —*L*

She sighed as Nathan's face flickered in her mind—a shadow of a memory just beyond reach.

A moment later, the map glowed. Arthur's reply unfolded across the parchment:

> *Sounds like a Hypnos Inhibitor? Is this for real?*
> —*A*

Lilith shook her waterbub and scribbled again.

> *It seems like it.*
> *—L*

> *You're full of surprises, Fletcher. See you soon.*
> *—A*

She smiled. Arthur had a peculiar way of making things feel a little less heavy.

Lilith glanced at the bracelet before taking a bite of her food, its warmth pressed against her skin. Packages didn't just drop from the sky. If it hadn't come from her friends, *who had given it to her? And why?*

Chapter Twenty-Three

RING SEEKERS

T he bracelet rested against Lilith's wrist like it belonged there. It didn't pinch. It didn't burn. It just sat beneath her sleeve, warm and quiet, while she headed toward the Agon Palladium with Jake at her side. *Was that how it was supposed to feel—or proof it wasn't real at all?*

Apprentices poured into the arena for the Ring Seekers challenge, their voices bouncing off the stadium walls, but Lilith kept scanning the crowd. Maybe whoever had left the bracelet was there. Maybe she could catch them watching.

Beside her, Jake looked like he had just as many questions as she did. But he stayed quiet.

"Fletcher. Hills," Arthur called from behind them.

Lilith turned and forced herself to breathe. "Hey."

"Arthur!" Jake clasped his hands under his chin. "Please tell me I'm not losing my mind. It really does look like the real thing, right?"

Arthur's gaze flicked once to Lilith's sleeve. "Not now. We're about to start." Then his eyes moved between them. "Hypnos or not, do your best—and don't get hurt."

From the yellow lineup, Adrien waved, surrounded by other kids as usual. Lilith and Jake waved back.

"Okay. Good luck, you two," Arthur said.

"You too," Lilith said, managing a grin. "Not that you actually need it."

"All competitors, head to your designated spots," Principal Stewart's voice rang through the stadium.

After fist-bumping each other, Arthur strode toward the green line, Jake went to the blue, and Lilith headed to the red line, taking a spot behind Hannah.

There were fourteen colors, with five apprentices assigned to each section. The first goal was straightforward: find the hidden ring and wear it. Only the apprentice wearing the ring would advance to the second—and final—part of the challenge: one-on-one combat.

Energy shields hummed to life, sealing each colored section into an isolated dome. The arena fell silent. Even the spectators in the bleachers leaned forward, anticipation thick in the air.

A loud gong echoed through the space—the challenge had begun.

The red dome around Lilith plunged into total darkness. Gasps echoed around her as apprentices scrambled like startled fish. Lilith took a steadying breath and activated her Drakon-sight, letting the outlines of the world appear in the dark. Now she could see. One apprentice sank into the ground; another conjured fireballs, illuminating the shifting shadows near him. The other two sprinted off, casting spells in every direction.

Lilith stayed put, scanning for anything—or anyone—out of place. The bushes were empty. No sign of creatures. A flash of lightning shot upward from across the dome. There—a tiny sparkle flickered between two tree branches whenever the Zeus apprentice hurled electricity skyward.

Lilith teleported, landing exactly where she needed. But the Zeus apprentice materialized inches in front of her.

"Too slow," he said with a smirk, snatching the sparkle. Lilith's heart sank until he growled, flipping the object in his hand—a coin. A fake. "Ugh, annoying tricks!" he snapped, flicking it into the air before teleporting away.

A decoy. Lilith exhaled, jumping down from the branch, barely noticing the sting of her scraped knee. She still had a chance.

Minutes dragged on. Lilith blasted dozens of areas with Life Powder, turning over rocks, shaking leaves, digging through dirt—still no ring.

Lilith dropped to one knee and scanned the other four apprentices inside the red dome. Another lightning bolt struck the center of the dome, raced down a metal pole, and vanished into a black box at its base. Lilith frowned, standing up and taking a cautious step forward. Another bolt. And another. She hurled a pulse of Life Powder at the black box. It burst with a sharp crack, and the darkness shattered with it. Daylight flooded the dome, though Lilith wasn't sure if she had made things better or killed her Drakon-sight advantage.

Five other domes had also cleared—green, yellow, blue, purple, and pink. Lilith's gaze snapped back to the center of the red arena. A floating apprentice soared toward the towering pole at the heart of the field. Perched at the very top, another sparkle. Lilith's hands shot up, frantically reclaiming Life Powder she'd scattered for the black box.

Hannah darted past Lilith, her hands a blur as she conjured a portal beneath the ring. Just before a second-year could snatch it, the jewel vanished into the swirling void. Lilith's heart pounded, another portal snapping open above Hannah's head. Before Hannah could grab the ring, an energy arrow shot through the air, knocking it away.

"Riiing!" someone yelled, and every head turned as the jewel tumbled to the ground. A stampede followed—but Lilith didn't move. Instead, she formed a thin tendril of Life Powder and guided it toward the ring, wrapping it in a shimmer of gold. Apprentices lunged, collided, and fought tooth and nail around it, but Lilith held her breath and grounded herself. Beneath her feet, roots stirred, whispering back. The earth swallowed the orb whole.

With a slow, steady breath, Lilith lifted her hands. The soil cracked. A glimmer broke through—the ring, still cradled in Life Powder. It drifted straight onto her finger.

For a split second, she could only stare, disbelieving. Then the arena erupted in cheers, the roar of voices crashing over her like a wave.

A sharp tone rang out, followed by Principal Stewart's booming voice. "Red dome winner: Lilith Fletcher!"

Hannah popped beside her. "Fair is fair," she said quietly.

Lilith managed a smile before being called to join the seats encircling the domes to wait for the remaining apprentices to finish. Arthur, Jake, and Adrien were already there, winners. They had probably finished their domes before hers was even down.

After nearly an hour of intense competition, the final fourteen winners were set—ready to face the last part of the challenge. Principal Stewart stepped forward, and the crowd fell silent before he even spoke. As he congratulated the apprentices, Professors Lewis and Moonlit lifted their hands—magic pulsing from their fingertips, the ground rumbling. Stone shifted, reshaping itself and molding the battlefield into something new before the crowd's eyes.

When the magic settled, the arena had been split into seven sections by energy walls, each marked by a large, round button at its center. Principal Stewart's voice carried through the air. "As you all know, the powers of the brothers Castor and Pollux were interconnected. They shared their immortality and mortality. And for the purpose of this challenge, so do the rings you are wearing. One cannot function without its pair."

Lilith's fingers curled slightly around her own ring.

"Now that you've secured half of what you need, you will face an opponent for the other half. Only seven of you will emerge victorious. The rules are straightforward: your opponent—drawn at random—must, somehow, press the surrender button between the two of you. You may use both offensive and defensive skills," he continued. "Ready? Proceed to your assigned spots."

Lilith's stomach twisted. Christopher Fox, a third-year Ares student, stood across her. He wore the top half of his brown hair in a small tie, with the bottom half shaved close—almost Viking-like. His expression was sharp, and his presence alone screamed serious competition. He looked as intense as Arthur when something actually mattered.

She gulped. Her fingers brushed against her sleeve, feeling the metal of the Hypnos Inhibitor hidden beneath. *Please be the real deal,* she begged internally. It would be really helpful against an Ares apprentice with mind-control skills.

Principal Stewart's voice boomed, each word drawn out, dripping with suspense. "Three..." The air in the arena thickened. "Two..." Lilith's heartbeat pounded in her ears, her palms damp with sweat. "One..." She locked eyes with Christopher. "Go!"

Flames roared to life in his hands, a fiery helm flickering into existence above his head as he hurled a fireball. Lilith dove to the side, rolling across the dirt as the heat seared the air. Flames crackled, leaving a blackened scorch mark on the ground. Her breath hitched. He was fast.

Christopher smirked, flames licking up his arms. "Running already?"

Lilith exhaled through her teeth and teleported behind a nearby pillar. The cool stone pressed against her back, a relief against the heat surrounding her—she needed a plan.

In the section beside hers, Jake crouched behind a tree, swiftly opening a portal before his opponent. A second portal shimmered directly over the surrender button in his section. His opponent stumbled through—and landed square on it. He made it look effortless.

The crowd erupted in cheers, excitement pulsing through the stadium. One of the seven seats behind the sectioned arenas lit up with J. Hills. Jake headed there, chin up, and Lilith couldn't have been prouder.

A sudden explosion yanked Lilith's attention back. A fireball smashed the stone pillar beside her, fracturing it with a deafening crack. She dodged the falling rubble, throwing herself into a roll before darting between obstacles.

Lilith stayed low, heart pounding. *If she could just get close enough to use Life Powder...* But Christopher wasn't giving her a chance. He stomped the ground, and fire exploded outward in a shockwave. Lilith's eyes widened—no time to run. She leaped.

Pushing off a boulder, she flipped over the flames just as they surged beneath her. Heat clawed at her heels, a blistering wave chasing her mid-motion. She landed in a crouch, breathless but unharmed.

Shaking off the rush of fear, Lilith teleported to a bush beside Christopher. She barely had time to shape Life Powder before a blast erupted from Christopher's chest, scattering everything like dust in the wind. "Good try," he said, cracking his knuckles. "But not good enough."

He slammed his hands together—*FWOOSH*. A towering firewall roared behind her. Then another. And another. They weren't just barriers—they were moving walls of flame, closing in, herding her toward the surrender button.

Lilith's pulse thundered in her ears. If she didn't act now, it was over. Drakon-sight slid into place, sharpening the edges of the flames, the angle of Christopher's stance, every twitch before he moved. He expected her to panic. But she wasn't giving up. Lilith waited, breath burning in her chest, and, just as the fire closed in, she teleported, reappearing high above Christopher, ready to strike.

He growled, head snapping up with eerie precision. *How did he know?* Lilith tensed, sweat trickling down her temple as she descended. He wasn't just fast. He was trained, powerful, and furious.

Christopher's eyes darkened. "Let's see how well you fight when you're under my control." He raised one hand, two fingers aimed straight at her. A red pulse shot from his fingertips like an arrow finding its mark.

Lilith braced herself—but the pulse struck the air around her wrist and scattered like sparks. Her eyes widened. *The bracelet. It worked.*

Frustration flashed across his face. He dropped low and slammed both hands into the ground. *BOOM!*

A fiery shockwave ripped through the earth, smashing into Lilith like a wrecking ball. She barely had time to blink before she was hurled backward, tumbling across scorched dirt. Gritting her teeth, she rolled to a stop, chest heaving. The world spun around her, everything blurred.

When she finally spotted Christopher, he was already on his feet—charging. Lilith's fingers brushed the ground, damp beneath the scorched surface, before she flung her hands upward.

Vines exploded from the earth, roses twisting around Christopher's legs. He grunted, staggering, balance tipping—she was close. So close. Just one more push.

But then she saw his face. The wince in his expression as thorns pierced his skin. He was hurting. Lilith's breath caught, a flicker of hesitation creeping in. That was all Christopher needed. *A flicker.*

He snarled, tearing against the vines. "Cheap trick, Grim Wannabe!" His voice was raw with frustration. Fire erupted around him, devouring the vines in an instant. Ash spiraled in the air. Lilith's knees turned to jelly. She flinched, raising an arm against the wave of heat rushing toward her.

Christopher's eyes locked on hers—fierce, unrelenting. He lunged forward. A shockwave of air crashed into Lilith's chest. The force tore the breath from her lungs as her back slammed against the surrender button. The world tilted in slow motion.

Lilith lay there, stunned. She had lost. Christopher dusted bits of vine from his shoulders with an infuriating smirk. "I don't know what trick you pulled to keep me out of your head," he said, voice low, "but I wasn't about to lose to an unarmed first-year Looper. Not in my third year." His smirk sharpened. "Almost impressive. Too bad you're soft." He stepped back, eyes still burning. "Mercy costs points, Grim Wannabe." Then he turned and walked away.

The world buzzed like static. The cheers, the shouts, the other battles still raging—it all felt distant.

Lilith had *almost* won. She hated *almosts*. Losing sucked.

CHAPTER TWENTY-FOUR

BENEATH THE SURFACE

The feast after Ring Seekers was supposed to feel like a celebration. But it wasn't for Lilith.

"Hi, Rose," she said on her way to the dining hall. "How are you?"

"Rose good." Rose looked Lilith over from head to toe. "Lilith win?"

"No," Lilith said, forcing a smile. "But at least now I can drown my sorrows in hot chocolate."

"Sorry no win." Rose ruffled Lilith's hair with her heavy hand, then caught Lilith's hand in an awkward shake, like she had just remembered that was something people did. "But Lilith safe. Good."

Lilith blinked. "Yeah. I guess that's also something."

"Win next time," Rose said, nodding firmly before letting go.

Apprentices were called to the feast, and Rose waved before lumbering away. Lilith followed the crowd inside.

The hall glittered with golden-ring banners and platters stacked with ridiculous themed desserts. The seven winners sat in their marked seats at the start of the feast while Principal Stewart gave a short speech. Then apprentices crowded around them, laughing, cheering, and asking for every detail of every victory.

Lilith stabbed her fork into a croissant dipped in chocolate just as Christopher strolled by and winked at her.

"You were so close," Jake said, pouting as he sank into the seat beside her. Arthur took the chair on her other side.

Arthur raised an eyebrow. "What did the croissant do to you?"

Lilith blinked, forcing herself back to the present. "Sorry." She exhaled slowly and reached for a napkin. Her bracelet clinked against her cup, and she pressed her hand over her sleeve, as if that could hold the secret in place. "I still can't believe this thing saved me from Christopher's mind control. I have soooo many questions."

Arthur's gaze flicked toward her wrist. "You aren't the only one," he said, and Jake nodded.

Across the hall, Adrien laughed a bit too loudly, enjoying the attention as he reenacted his victory for a group of admirers. Lilith rolled her eyes. *Typical.* Then she scanned the rest of the room, unsure if she was looking for someone who could possibly have given her the bracelet—or if it was because she had this weird feeling she was being watched.

Principal Stewart, Professor Lewis, and Professor Thomas stood by the center tables, trading stories about past Ring Seekers challenges—the kind everyone still talked about years later. Lilith had probably never seen the dining hall so full. It was almost impossible to see all the way across the room. Her gaze drifted toward the entrance. A blue bird perched atop a statue, its head tilted.

Lilith frowned. *Was it looking at her?* She stretched her neck, but a group of apprentices crossed her line of sight. By the time she could see the entrance again, the bird was gone. She sat up straighter. "Did you see that? That was weird, right?" she whispered.

Arthur and Jake followed her gaze.

Jake leaned in. "See what?"

Lilith hesitated. "Mmm... never mind," she said, shaking her head and trying to focus on celebrating her friends instead of sulking over her loss.

The days after the Ring Seekers challenge blurred together. The winners reveled in their privileges while Lilith tried not to stare too hard from the sidelines. Exclusive training. Access to lost relics. Mentorships she had secretly been excited about—not as much as Jake, but still. All gone because she had hesitated.

It wasn't jealousy. Not exactly.

Lilith was proud of her friends. She was. But every time she saw one of the winners disappear for exclusive training or come back whispering about lost relics, disappointment curled tighter in her chest.

If she had been a little faster, or a little tougher...she could have won.

Maybe losing proved what she had been afraid of all along: Arthur and Jake would be better off with someone who could actually keep up.

Lilith tried not to dwell on it. Instead of following that dark path, she threw herself into the restricted library, making the most of the guest passes Adrien kept tossing her way from his winner perks—since, according to him, *he had better things to do.* She combed through ancient texts on the Fates ritual, searching for anything that might help her find a Mnemosyne apprentice capable of restoring her memories. Most days, she, Arthur, and Jake sat for hours, poring over dusty tomes and scribbling notes.

Arthur had also become fixated on the Cellar of Lost and Found, where each winner was allowed to claim an artifact that had gone unclaimed for at least a decade. Adrien, Jake, and Arthur all searched for a python scale or a minotaur hair before choosing their artifacts, but they came up empty.

One afternoon, Lilith sat in the dining hall, idly stirring a bowl of soup she had no intention of finishing, mostly avoiding a call with her family. Since she had found out about Nathan, the words felt heavy on her tongue. How could she keep pretending her brother had never existed? Shouldn't her dad be allowed to know he had a son, too? She barely noticed when Arthur arrived.

"Here," he said, pulling something from his pocket—an iridescent blue-green scale with a copper tinge.

Lilith's eyes widened. "How—how did you get this?"

"I didn't want to say anything before, in case it fell through," he said, rubbing the back of his neck, "but my grandfather knew someone who owed him a favor. The man runs an antique shop for rare artifacts. So, I put in a request a few months back and managed to secure it through a trade."

Lilith stared at him. "Arthur—this is insane. Thank you so much! I'm so happy I didn't have to drag Kallista into this mess."

Arthur shrugged. "Thank my grandfather."

Lilith smiled. "I don't think I can ever repay you for everything—or Jake, for that matter."

Arthur met her gaze, steady. "There's no debt here, Fletcher."

She bit the inside of her cheek. She almost hugged him, then remembered this was Arthur. So she held herself back with everything she had and grinned instead.

Jake arrived moments later, balancing three plates, a wrapped sandwich, and his backpack. He barely had time to set everything down before a sharp voice cut through the air.

"Arthur." Aidan Owens stood at the entrance of the dining hall. The entire room quieted down. "Come." His tone was crisp, leaving no room for argument.

Jake jumped, nearly dropping one of the plates. But Arthur didn't flinch. He nodded to Lilith and Jake, then followed his father outside.

Lilith and Jake exchanged glances; they didn't need words. Slipping out, they followed them from a distance. Jake unwrapped a sandwich and took a huge bite, which would have looked ridiculous if his face hadn't been so strangely blank, like the worry hadn't quite reached him. Lilith shot him a look. He chewed, unbothered until they stopped just outside one of the meeting rooms.

Aidan's voice seeped through the thick stone walls even with the door closed. "What were you thinking, contacting him? Your grandfather?"

Arthur's voice was calm but tight. "I needed advice."

"Advice?" Aidan scoffed. "Advice?" There was a pause, then his tone sharpened. "You think you need guidance from that fool? I've already told you that you're forbidden to speak to him. Do you understand that, or will we have a problem again?"

"I understand, Father," Arthur answered, quieter this time.

Lilith's stomach tightened. *The scale. Arthur had contacted his grandfather for her, hadn't he?*

Aidan's voice dropped to a low growl. "And you'd better not be lying to me, boy. If I find out you went behind my back—"

"It won't happen again," Arthur cut in, his voice steady.

Aidan's silence was heavier than his words. Then, low and cold, "It better not. You're still nothing but a disappointment."

Lilith stiffened when the door swung open. Aidan stormed past them, barely sparing a glance. As if he didn't care they were there. Arthur followed a moment later, expression unreadable, his movements controlled.

"Not now," Arthur said, raising a hand to Lilith when she opened her mouth. And he didn't stop walking, vanishing down the hall.

Lilith stared at the empty corridor, stomach twisting. "How could anyone treat their son like that?" she muttered. "That's wrong. Aidan is straight-up cruel."

Jake sighed, running a hand through his hair. "Nicole might be the one endymionized, but I've always thought there was more to the story than people say."

"Nicole-who?" She blinked.

"Arthur's mom," he replied.

Lilith lifted both eyebrows, shifting her weight. "I'm gonna need more than that. I'm lost."

Jake dropped onto a nearby bench, his voice lowering. "Arthur's mom. Nicole Owens. She was endymionized years ago after his little sister, Sophie, died. Arthur was only four, I think."

Lilith sat beside him. "His sister died? How? And why am I only hearing this now?"

Jake pressed his lips together. "Because people don't talk about it. Not around Arthur." He looked down at his hands. "The official story is that Nicole killed her."

"What?" The word escaped before she could stop it. "His mom killed his sister?" Lilith rubbed her face.

"Yes, and as a sentence, she was sent to Poine's Penitentiary. Can you imagine being trapped inside your nightmares, just lying in a room for the rest of your life? Nowhere to escape to. No hope." He cracked his neck. "My uncle works in Nicole's ward. He told me Arthur visits her, but she's gone—trapped in her mind, with no idea what's going on."

"I had no idea," she whispered, the weight of it settling in. "C-can she ever come back?"

"Homicide is a lifetime sentence." Jake paused, as if the thought had reached him late. "I probably shouldn't be telling you this."

Lilith swallowed hard. Arthur had a dead sister, a mother trapped in nightmares, and a father who treated him like a mistake. The world got heavier.

Jake stretched, yawning. "We should head to our rooms. You and Arthur have the Minotaur encounter tomorrow. You don't want to be late."

Lilith frowned at him. "How are you so calm?"

He popped the last bite of his sandwich into his mouth and lifted his arm, pulling back his sleeve to reveal the empathy blocker. "I snapped it on as soon as I saw Aidan. I can't feel much right now," he said, voice flat. "Which is exactly the point."

Her gaze lingered on him, noticing his usual brightness was gone.

He shrugged, standing up. "Anyway, we should get some sleep. I'll meet you guys tomorrow. You don't want to be half-dead at dawn."

They walked in silence. Lilith's thoughts spiraled about what she'd learned about Arthur. It was too heavy to shrug off.

Just as the Zeus Wing doors opened, Jake stopped short and slapped his forehead. "I forgot my backpack in the dining hall," he groaned.

"Oh, let's go get it," she said, turning back.

"Nah. Don't worry about it. You go to sleep. It's late, and I'm not the one facing a baby Minotaur tomorrow." He smirked, but it never quite reached his eyes.

"You sure?"

"Yeah. Don't worry," he said, already jogging off, weaving through the halls.

Lilith headed to her room. She didn't take long to crawl into bed after that, but sleep stayed far away.

Her brother. The ritual. Christopher's victory over her. The possibility of finding a minotaur's hair the following morning. Aidan's crushing voice. Arthur's silent pain. All of it followed her into the dark.

CHAPTER TWENTY-FIVE

INTO THE MAZE

I t was too early for anyone to be this awake, but Lilith's nerves had apparently mistaken sunrise for a battle horn. She pulled open the curtains and watched golden light spill over the Academy grounds. Today was the long-awaited maze encounter, and maybe her last chance to get the final ingredient for the ritual: a minotaur's hair.

Before leaving, Lilith tightened her sleeve around the Hypnos Inhibitor—she hadn't taken it off since the Ring Seekers challenge. Her hand hovered over the door handle, but she hesitated. *Would this be the last time she saw her room?* A strange ache settled in her chest as she stepped out.

The hallways buzzed with students, their excitement louder than their footsteps. Everyone loved the end-of-year special challenges and classes. She found Arthur on the way to the Andron Room where the students from Intro to Mythical Creatures would gather for breakfast.

Lilith and Arthur filled their plates alongside their classmates. The options were noticeably more limited than the usual dining hall spread—probably chosen to boost stamina. Lilith took a bite of her food but then stopped, her gaze drifting to the floor.

"Fletcher," Arthur called. He shifted, adjusting the strap of his bag like it suddenly needed fixing and cleared his throat. "When this is over..." His eyes flicked away. "It won't be the same around here."

Lilith's fork paused halfway to her mouth.

Before she could say anything, Arthur's brow furrowed. He looked past her shoulder. "Wait—is that Hills?"

Lilith turned. "It is Jake!" She scratched her forehead. "Jake! I thought you weren't allowed near the maze—or this class at all?"

Jake hesitated, unusually quiet. His gaze fixed on Lilith with a strange intensity, like he was waiting for her to do something.

"Are you all right?" she asked.

A faint warmth stirred beneath her sleeve, then vanished. Lilith's eyes darted across the room before she could stop herself, searching for Christopher. *Was he trying something already?* But Christopher was nowhere she could see.

"Uh, yeah," Jake said slowly, a fraction too late. Lilith turned back to him as he added, "They needed a hand with something." His eyes flicked around the room instead of landing on hers.

Arthur's eyes narrowed. "Really?" Lilith wondered if they were in a fight she didn't know about, but the bell rang before she could ask—the Minotaur encounter was about to start. "Never mind. Ready?" he asked.

"Ready isn't quite the right word," Lilith said, flattening her lips. "But... as ready as I'll ever be, I guess. Not sure if you-know-what will be useful this time, but I still have it with me."

"Huh?" Jake blinked. "Oh. Right. Good." He cracked his knuckles and glanced toward Professor Moonlit and Professor Lewis, shoulders hunched. "I'll see you later," he said, as if he was about to get in trouble.

"See you soon... I guess?" Lilith muttered even though he was already gone.

"He was acting weird, right?" Arthur asked. "I mean, even for Hills?"

"I'm glad I wasn't the only one who thought that," Lilith murmured. "I thought you guys had a fight." Arthur shook his head in response. "Maybe he didn't actually convince Professor Moonlit and just sneaked in?"

Arthur shrugged. "Maybe."

"Everyone, form a line over here," Professor Lewis called. He was assisting Professor Moonlit along with Professor Goldsmith.

"And remember: don't let the minotaur eat the food you're carrying. Don't let anyone else take your puzzle piece. As soon as you reach the exit door, assemble any remaining pieces, and it will unlock so you can exit. I hope this is an enriching experience for each one of you," Professor Moonlit added, her voice commanding yet warm. "Now, now, each of you will start at your designated cave entrance, but you'll all be positioned at an equal distance from the exit—and the minotaur."

Professor Moonlit's deep blue and silver robe, adorned with symbols, shimmered as she raised her wrist. The Hecate wheel marked on her skin—a maze with three distinct spirals connected to a six-sided star—lit up while the students lined up in front of her. The pitch-black door beside her shifted, no longer solid but an open passageway.

"I guess it's time." Lilith inhaled deeply.

"Let's get you that minotaur hair," Arthur whispered, clipping his puzzle piece securely to his belt.

"What if we can't get it?"

Arthur raised an eyebrow. "Who are you, and what have you done with the Fletcher I know?"

"I'm serious. It's a labyrinth! It took me two weeks just to figure out how to get to my dorm from the Great Hall," she muttered. "And... I couldn't beat Christopher—how am I supposed to handle a minotaur?"

"Hey," he said, steady. "Focus on protecting your puzzle piece and your food pouch—hold onto those, and we'll find each other in there," he reassured. "And we're all after a minotaur hair—even Fjeld. Odds are we might end up with enough to make a wig."

"You're a really good friend," she said, softer than she meant to. "And, Arthur? I'll miss you too." For once, he didn't have a sharp answer ready.

Lilith stepped through the threshold and into the cave. Behind her, the portal sealed with the rumble of a rocky wall.

Darkness swallowed her whole, but Lilith's Drakon-sight activated instinctively, sharpening the world around her. The cave walls pulsed with a faint, eerie energy. She had been warned they were cursed—designed to drain magic from anyone inside. When she glanced up, a question nagged at her: *how could the ceiling be transparent from the outside, letting spectators watch, yet remain this dark within?*

Golden initials glowed on Lilith's left palm, one line at a time—the sixteen students attempting to outsmart the minotaur. She touched her own name, hoping it would stay there long enough. "Here we go." Lilith exhaled as the shield before her dropped, marking the official start of the Minotaur encounter. "All right, it's just a baby minotaur," she whispered.

Moving cautiously, she scanned the floor for minotaur hair while guarding her puzzle piece and the pouch of food at her hip. Every turn, calm, silent. Until it wasn't. *Clip-clop. Clip-clop.*

Lilith's stomach tightened.

She pushed off the ground, floating high above just as the heavy gallop grew louder. Then the creature emerged, twice her size, its muscular frame covered in thick black fur. Its polished horns gleamed in the low light as it sniffed the air beneath her.

That was not a baby. Or if it was, Lilith wanted a serious conversation with whoever named things around here.

"Hun-gry," it snorted.

Go away, Lilith begged silently.

If the cave walls hadn't blocked teleporting beyond the maze's boundaries, there was a very real chance Lilith would have chickened out right then. But she could only teleport within the maze, and only to spots she had already visited.

"Food," the minotaur growled, nostrils flaring.

Lilith clenched her jaw, scanning for a route to escape. Then the minotaur shook its head and galloped away. Lilith stayed still for a few seconds, just in case the minotaur was smart enough to try to trick her, but a loud thud echoed instead. Lilith turned just in time to see the minotaur slam into Ella Koskinen—Kami's friend, gifted by Poseidon—stealing the food pouch from her waist.

Lilith's palm warmed as the letters E.K. pulsed and disappeared from the golden list. A portal opened beneath Ella, swallowing her whole while the minotaur devoured the food in the pouch. Ella's puzzle piece hovered, unclaimed. Lilith stiffened—if abandoned puzzle pieces naturally drifted toward the exit, could she follow one to find her way out? It was her best shot.

One by one, students' initials disappeared, shrinking the list. Every elimination left fewer targets for the minotaur, every second in there drained more of her strength—but she pushed through. By the time Hannah's name vanished, only four students remained—Arthur, Adrien, Ruby, and Lilith. She swallowed hard.

"Oh, come on!" Lilith whispered in frustration when the puzzle piece she had been following veered into a swampy corridor. Teleporting from one dry patch to another, she gritted her teeth. Each jump sapped more of her energy. The cursed walls were doing their job. As she crossed the swamp, Ruby's initials disappeared. Lilith's chest tightened. Arthur and Adrien were still there. *But for how long? And had they found any minotaur hair?*

At last, the swamp ended. Lilith wiped sweat from her forehead and teleported past the final patch of mud.

Then—she saw it. Ella's puzzle piece drifted to a stop near the door, joining the pieces already waiting there. The center of the maze. The exit was right there, sealed and waiting for the last of the pieces. Lilith's heart jumped. This had to be where the minotaur had started. She dropped to her knees and let Drakon-sight take over. The cave floor snapped into focus—cracks, pebbles, dust, maybe even hair. If anyone could find a needle in a haystack, it was her.

"Lilith? Where are you?" Jake's voice echoed through the maze.

Jake? She frowned. *What was he doing inside the cave? He wasn't supposed to be here. But that might be good, right? One more ally?*

Lilith turned toward the sound just as Arthur stepped out from another passage. Lilith's face lit up. "You made it! And Jake is here? Wait—I made it? How did I survive that giant baby cow?" She let out a breathless laugh.

"Wait." Arthur grabbed her sleeve, his eyes narrowing. "Something isn't right."

"Perceptive, aren't we?" Jake's voice was... off. *Too thin. Too light. Too—*

Lilith froze.

Jake lifted his hand. With a lazy flick of his wrist, a massive rock hurtled toward her. Lilith's instincts screamed. She barely had time to react before Arthur shot a bolt of lightning at the boulder, reducing it to dust. "You again?"

Jake's hair turned blonde. His voice warped, distorting into something sharper, higher. "You're making me angry." His wrist glowed, but the usual Apollo mark was gone. Instead, the symbol of Hera pulsed where his Apollo mark should've been.

221

Arthur tensed. "What do you want?" His voice was low, dangerous.

"You already know what I want," the not-Jake said smoothly. His body was shifting—stretching, thinning. His hair lengthened into golden waves. His face sharpened into something eerily familiar.

Lilith's breath caught. She knew that face. "You're Nathan's friend," she whispered.

The woman smirked, rolling her shoulders as the last of the transformation settled. "Teammate." She adjusted the sleeves of her now-fitted tunic. "I'm Elizabeth Hindley."

Lilith's blood turned cold. "Wait—where is Jake?"

Elizabeth grinned, tilting her head. "Oh, him?" She traced a lazy finger through the air. "He served his purpose. I don't need him anymore."

Lilith's pulse hammered. "What did you do to him?"

Elizabeth's smile thinned. "He screamed for you, you know." Lilith's world seemed to tilt as Elizabeth took one step forward, voice soft as poison. "Then he stopped."

Something inside Lilith went cold. She took a step back, fists clenching. "You know the teachers are watching us, right? They'll be here any second."

Elizabeth laughed. "You think so? Because I think they're too busy trying to figure out why they can't see through the maze walls right now." She grinned. "So let's make the best of this alone time, shall we?"

Arthur lifted his hands, lightning crackling between his fingers.

"Oh, that's cute." Elizabeth crossed her arms, completely unbothered. "You do know I can control lightning too, right? Hera made sure I could borrow a few of Zeus's favorite tricks. Whatever you're planning—it won't work, kiddo."

Arthur lunged. In a blink, he knocked Lilith to the ground and hurled a bolt into the ceiling above Elizabeth. The cave trembled. A massive boulder broke loose, crashing down toward them. Lilith flinched, ready to teleport—but his Aegis shimmered into place just in time. The boulder smashed against it, breaking apart in a cloud of dust.

As the debris settled, Arthur lowered the shield and staggered to the side.

"Arthur?" Lilith scrambled to her feet, reaching for him. "Are you okay?"

"I'm fine," he muttered, voice tight. "Hopefully, Hindley isn't."

Lilith's pulse raced as she scanned the destruction. "Where did she go?"

Arthur's body stiffened. His head tilted unnaturally.

"I'm right here," a voice purred.

Lilith's stomach twisted. Elizabeth's hand rested on Arthur's shoulder, nails pressing ever so slightly into his jacket while his emerald eyes had gone eerily vacant, glassy, and unfocused. She wasn't just standing behind him. *She was controlling him.*

"Arthur?" Lilith whispered.

But when he spoke, the voice that came out wasn't his. It was distant and hollow, with Elizabeth's venom curled around every word.

"Unfortunately, Arthur's a little busy right now."

Lilith's breath shallowed. Mind control was bad. Arthur under mind control was worse.

Chapter Twenty-Six

PUPPETEER

A rthur moved like someone had tied invisible strings to his bones and pulled too hard. His fingers twitched. Sparks snapped between his fingers, bright and wrong.

Lilith took one step back. "Arthur?"

His eyes stayed glassy. Elizabeth's smile stretched across his face, which was officially one of the worst things Lilith had ever seen. And considering the year she'd had, that was saying something.

"I didn't plan this," Elizabeth said through him. Arthur's voice came out hollow, scraped clean of everything that made it his. "I wanted you to die like you were supposed to. Quick. Simple. But everyone kept interfering."

Arthur's hand jerked upward. Lightning crawled over his knuckles. Lilith's fingers twitched toward her pendant. "What did I ever do to you?"

His mouth curled, but it wasn't his smile. "You existed," Elizabeth hissed. "Your brother was supposed to take your Life Powder. He refused. Then he killed my best friend to protect you."

The words hit harder than lightning. *Nathan refused to take her Life Powder? Was that why he'd been there the night of Lilith's fourteenth birthday?*

Arthur's arm snapped forward. Lilith dove. The bolt exploded against the wall behind her. Pebbles stung her arms. Dust filled her mouth.

Lilith coughed. "You're insane!"

Elizabeth laughed with Arthur's voice. "Oh, sweetie. You have no idea."

Another bolt lit the cave. Lilith teleported behind a boulder, heart hammering so hard it felt like it was trying to escape. Elizabeth could control Arthur, which meant she had his speed, his lightning, his Aegis. Perfect. Wonderful. Terrible.

Lilith shaped Life Powder into a spear, aiming for Elizabeth's blind spot. Then came a sound that made every thought in her brain trip over itself.

Clomp. Clomp—the minotaur.

"Oh, come on," Lilith whispered. "Now?"

The creature stomped into the chamber, snorting hard enough to rattle dust from the ceiling. Elizabeth's head snapped toward it. Lilith threw the spear anyway.

For one beautiful second, it worked. Then Arthur's hand flew up, and his Aegis flashed into place. The spear burst against the shield, scattering Life Powder like golden dust.

"Fiddlesticks," Lilith muttered.

Arthur turned toward the minotaur. Lilith's stomach dropped. "No!"

Electricity crackled in his hands. Arthur hurled a bolt straight at the creature, but Lilith teleported between them on instinct, arms raised, dragging every scrap of Life Powder she could reach into a barrier.

Too slow. The world exploded.

A blinding flash swallowed her. Her vision turned white. Her ears rang with the roar of energy colliding. The force hurled her backward, heat searing her skin before she slammed into the cavern wall.

For a moment, everything blurred. Static buzzed in her head. Her limbs felt far away, like they belonged to someone else. The air smelled of scorched stone.

Move. Lilith forced her eyes open, blinking through the haze. The minotaur calf had bolted, kicking up dust as it vanished down a winding tunnel. Smart move. She wished she could do the same.

A groan snapped her attention back. Arthur lay crumpled on the ground, unmoving. His Aegis had shattered, its protective magic flickering out like dying embers. He must have been caught in the blast too.

Lilith's heart pounded. "Arthur?"

No response.

Then, through the thinning smoke, Elizabeth stepped forward—completely unharmed. Worse, she was smiling.

"Well," she said, dusting off her shoulder. "That was fun. For me, anyway."

Lilith pushed herself onto shaking arms, fingers digging into the dirt, searching for leftover Life Powder. *There had to be something she could do.*

Elizabeth sighed dramatically. "You know, this really would've been easier if Nathan had just let things happen."

Arthur stirred. *No.*

With unnatural stiffness, he forced himself to his feet. His movements were jerky and wrong. His eyes—usually sharp enough to cut through stone—were dull. Hollow. Trapped.

Lilith's pulse slammed against her ribs. *No, no, no.*

Elizabeth looked delighted. "Round two?" Arthur's hands crackled.

Lilith couldn't keep dodging him. Not like this. Not while every teleport scraped more energy out of her bones.

"Arthur, stop!" she yelled. Not even a flicker of recognition.

Elizabeth leaned against a stone pillar like she was watching a show. "Oh, I bet you thought you could save him. I thought I could save my friend too—until Nathan killed him."

Lilith's fists clenched. "Let. Him. Go."

"No can do," Elizabeth replied. Arthur lunged.

Lilith ducked, rolling across the floor before teleporting a short distance away. Her breath tore in and out of her chest. Her magic was draining fast. If she didn't act now, she'd be too weak to fight back at all.

Her hand brushed her sleeve. *The Hypnos Inhibitor. Of course.*

No time to second-guess. She unclasped it from her own wrist, teleported behind Arthur, and snapped it around his.

A pulse of blinding gold erupted from the bracelet. Arthur jerked violently. Sparks ripped across his arms, then shattered outward like broken glass. Elizabeth's hold snapped.

His eyes cleared. His knees buckled. Lilith barely caught him before he hit the ground. She dropped beside him, one hand gripping his shoulder.

"Arthur?" she called.

His eyes fluttered open, unfocused but familiar.

Elizabeth snarled and hurled lightning toward them. Lilith didn't think. She threw a streak of Life Powder through the bolt instead, cutting it apart before it reached Arthur. The force shook her arms all the way to her shoulders.

And all Lilith could hear was: *He screamed for you. Then he stopped.*

Something inside her cracked open. The ground beneath Elizabeth trembled. Lilith raised both hands, but it didn't feel like casting. It felt like the cave itself had heard her rage and answered first.

The stone split. Thick vines burst upward, twisting around Elizabeth's legs, her waist, her arms.

Bell-shaped flowers bloomed along the vines, too pretty for something that wrong. Dark berries swelled at their centers.

Elizabeth's smile vanished. She flared lightning, trying to burn through the roots, but the flowers burst. A cloud of shimmering spores rolled over her like silver smoke. Then she coughed once. And again.

Her struggles slowed. Lilith's breath came in sharp, broken pulls. She didn't think poison. She didn't think stop.

She thought of Jake screaming. Arthur falling. Nathan gone.

"Lilith..." Arthur's voice was barely there.

She froze, but the vines kept tightening.

"Lilith," Arthur rasped again.

Her stomach dropped. Reality snapped back into place.

Lilith gasped and ripped her hands back. The vines loosened at once, snapping free from her control as if they had been burned.

"Arthur?" she called, but he didn't answer.

He had passed out.

Lilith grabbed his hands, trying to drag him toward the exit, but he was too heavy. Of course he was too heavy. *Why were unconscious people always impossible?*

She cursed under her breath and unclipped his puzzle piece instead, wondering why a portal hadn't opened beneath him like it had for Ella.

A faint, familiar sound grew in the distance.

Clomp. Clomp.

"Not again. Not now," Lilith muttered.

Her head spun as she slotted Arthur's piece into the door. Her vision blurred. She blinked hard, trying to clear it, and glanced back.

Elizabeth lay motionless in the vines. *Had Lilith gone too far? Was she...breathing?*

The thought barely had time to land before instinct took over again. She forced herself to find the slot for her own puzzle piece.

Her knees buckled and she hit the ground hard. *Clomp, clomp. Clomp, clomp.* The hoofbeats grew closer.

"Just a hair..." she mumbled, a metallic taste filling her mouth.

The so-called baby minotaur stopped, sniffing the air. Lilith stretched out a trembling hand. The creature snorted—just out of reach.

Come on. Please. But her fingers closed on nothing.

She could barely see the door anymore. But they had to get out. Hair or no hair.

Gritting her teeth, she pressed her piece into place. *Click.* The door swung open.

The bleachers erupted in cheers as bright light poured in—too bright, too loud, too much.

Professor Moonlit's voice sounded distant. Muffled. Someone else rushed toward her. *Professor Thomas?*

Lilith's lips parted. She needed to say Arthur needed help. That Elizabeth was still there. That Jake—

"Arthur," she managed. And everything went black.

CHAPTER TWENTY-SEVEN

FRAGMENTS OF HOME

L ilith woke slowly, like her body had forgotten how to be
awake. The room was dim, thank the Fates, but her head still
throbbed with every heartbeat. Her arms felt heavy. Her mouth
tasted bitter. The air smelled sharp and clean—antiseptics, herbs,
and healing spells humming softly above her bed.

The infirmary. Again.

She groaned softly, turning her head. A familiar figure
slouched in the chair beside her bed, trying very hard to look
casual.

"Welcome back, sleepyhead," Arthur's voice broke through her foggy thoughts.

His sleeves were rolled up, revealing arms covered in scratches and bruises.

"Are you okay? How long have you been here?" she murmured, pushing herself up on her elbows.

Arthur let his hands rest on the armrests. "I'm fine. And not long."

"Liar," Professor Lewis's voice rang out as he entered the room. "He's been here for the past six hours," he added, clearly enjoying Arthur's discomfort, "driving Donna crazy by refusing to rest." He handed Arthur a paper bag before turning to Lilith.

Arthur huffed but didn't deny it.

Professor Lewis clapped his hands together. "Now—how's our favorite maze survivor feeling?"

Lilith blinked. The Minotaur encounter... she had completed it. But she didn't get the hair. Her expression faltered.

"Did I say something wrong?" Professor Lewis asked, slipping a hand into his pocket.

"No, no, I just—WAIT!" Lilith's pulse spiked as everything came rushing back. "Jake! He—he was Elizabeth!" She jolted upright, making the room tilt.

"Breathe, Miss Fletcher," Professor Lewis said firmly, steadying her shoulder before she toppled over. "It's okay. Arthur already filled us in about the cave—and Elizabeth."

Lilith's breath came in short bursts, her heart still hammering. "But—Jake—"

"He's fine," Professor Lewis assured her. "He wanted to be here when you woke up, but I thought it best if he waited outside—so you wouldn't think he was still Elizabeth." He winked.

Lilith's vision blurred with sudden tears. *Jake was okay. He was okay.* The fear that had been sitting in her chest finally cracked, and for one terrifying second, she thought she might sob in front of everyone.

"I thought—" Her throat tightened, a single tear slipping down her cheek. "I thought—"

Professor Lewis's voice softened. "He's safe."

Arthur exhaled sharply. "Not thanks to me."

Lilith turned toward him. His jaw was tight, his gaze fixed on his lap.

"Fletcher," Arthur said quietly, shaking his head. "I'm really sorry for attacking you." His voice dipped, heavy with guilt.

"Don't." She scooted forward on the bed, facing him fully. "Elizabeth attacked me, not you." She tilted her head, trying to catch his gaze. "I should be apologizing. She only got to you *because* of me."

Arthur's mouth pressed into a thin line.

Professor Thomas, who had been standing silently near the doorway, exchanged a glance with Professor Lewis before stepping forward.

"Well," Professor Lewis sighed, stretching. "I'd love to stay longer, but I have a meeting with a few officers waiting to interrogate me about Elizabeth."

Lilith's voice was barely above a whisper. "What... happened to her?"

"Well, she absorbed a lot of Deadly Nightshade," Professor Lewis explained. Lilith's breath caught. "You basically put her to sleep. For a few hours, at least."

It was like a crushing weight had lifted off her shoulders. "So... she's alive?"

"Yes, very much so," Professor Lewis confirmed. "And she'll have her gift deactivated, as she deserves, before being sent to Poine's Penitentiary to serve her sentence." Professor Lewis adjusted his sleeves and headed for the door. "I'll let Jake know you're awake. Oh, and I expect you to stop by my office once you're fully recovered." He glanced over his shoulder, arching a brow.

Lilith nodded, managing a small smile.

As the door shut behind him, Arthur let out a breath. "Well," he said, breaking the silence. "You did it, Fletcher."

"No." Lilith met his gaze. "We did it. I wouldn't be here if it weren't for you and Jake." Her lips pressed together. "I didn't get the hair, though. Maybe we can sweep the arena tomorrow?"

Arthur's expression shifted. "Well—" He reached for the paper bag Professor Lewis had given him and pulled out their crumpled, dirt-streaked uniforms. Then, almost casually, he reached into the pocket of his ruined jacket. "I did at least one thing right today."

A tuft of coarse, dark fur dangled from his fingers. Lilith's eyes widened. "NO WAY!" she squealed before yanking him into a hug.

Arthur stiffened. *Oh—right. This was Arthur.* But just as she started to pull away, he hugged her back.

"Hi," Jake said shyly from the doorway, his hands buried in his pockets.

"Jake!" she practically leaped from the bed and wrapped him in a hug too. "I'm so happy you're okay."

Jake chuckled. "Me too." His cheeks lifted in a smile. "I still can't believe Elizabeth stole my face."

"How did that even happen? Where were you?" Lilith asked, settling on the bed's edge.

Jake sighed, pulling a chair closer to Arthur. "Remember the night before the Minotaur encounter? We were heading to the dorms, and I went back for my backpack?"

Lilith nodded.

"Well, after I got it, I heard someone crying for help from the supply room. I opened the door—" he grimaced. "—all I saw was a bolt coming at my face." Jake rubbed his arm. "By the time I came to, Elizabeth was already in my head." He glanced between them. "I'm sorry."

"You're not to blame," Lilith said firmly, her gaze flicking to Arthur. "Neither of you."

Professor Thomas stepped out to gather more herbs. Once she was gone, Lilith scratched her forehead. "Aren't we supposed to be safe inside the school's barrier?"

"A dumb student brought Elizabeth in as a guest," Arthur muttered, tapping his fingers on the chair's armrest.

Lilith blinked. "Who in their right mind would invite that lady in?"

Jake sighed. "She disguised herself as an injured blue jay—and Liam welcomed her."

Lilith tilted her head as the memory of the bird from the feast flashed back. *Could that have been Elizabeth?*

"You're right: no outsiders can break the barrier, but guests can enter with permission. Elizabeth hurt herself for real to sell the act. Liam said he brought her in weeks ago," Jake added, shaking his head. "She must've been waiting, recovering, and planning to go after you."

Arthur's fingers curled again. "Liam López just made the dumbest mistake in the Academy's history."

Jake shot him a look. "Don't be harsh, Arthur. Liam's gifted by Artemis—helping animals is second nature. He thought he was saving something," he said. "Anyway, he's in detention for an entire semester."

Arthur wrinkled his nose, but before he could respond, a harsh voice cut through the room.

"You." Aidan Owens stood in the doorway, his imposing figure casting a long shadow across the floor.

Lilith flinched slightly.

"Father." Arthur stiffened like a soldier.

"M-Mister Aidan. I mean—Mister Owens." Jake looked about as comfortable as a first-year forced to spar with Muck the Hammer.

Aidan's gaze never wavered. "You let yourself be controlled?" His tone was dry, sharp, cutting the air like a blade. "Why am I not surprised?"

Lilith snapped. "What's wrong with you?" She stepped forward, praying her knees wouldn't buckle.

Arthur's head whipped toward her. Jake looked mortified.

Aidan's dark eyes slowly shifted over to her, for the first time ever. *She probably shouldn't have said that.* His black shoes, perfectly polished, made no sound against the floor. "Aren't you a nosy one?" His voice was even colder than before—*how was that possible?*

Lilith squared her shoulders, refusing to shrink away. Aidan's gaze darkened further.

"Move." His tone sent a shiver down her spine. "I came to deal with my son, not an impertinent little thing like you."

Her fingers curled into fists, but Arthur stepped forward, a hand on her shoulder, gently moving her aside. "How can I help you, Father?" His voice was calm. Collected. Too composed—but his knuckles had whitened.

Aidan scoffed. "As if you could do anything useful."

Lilith growled under her breath. Arthur subtly raised a hand behind his back—a silent signal.

"Come. Now. I don't have all night." Aidan barely glanced back as he strode to the exit.

Arthur took a step forward, but Lilith's fingers gripped his sleeve. "Don't," she whispered.

He met her eyes, his expression gentle. "I'll be fine," he said, giving her a tiny nod before turning away and following his father out of the infirmary.

Silence fell heavily. Neither Lilith nor Jake spoke, both staring at the door as if staring hard enough might make Arthur come back. Lilith frowned, a pit forming in her stomach. *There had to be a way to help Arthur.*

Before the tension crushed her, a familiar voice broke the quiet.

"Hello? Everyone decent? Did someone die?" Adrien popped his head in.

"Adrien," she greeted, shaking her head, trying to regain focus. "Come on in."

"Just came by to say it's a pity I didn't get to beat you, Feisty." His rosy cheeks lifted, bright eyes shining.

Jake giggled, stepping aside to let Adrien pass. Lilith crossed her arms. "Do the math. I beat Elizabeth, who beat you."

"Burn!" Jake laughed.

Adrien tipped an imaginary hat. "Touché. You are making this a habit now." Then his grin widened. "I come bearing gifts." He opened his fist, revealing a strand of minotaur hair.

Jake's eyes widened. "No way!"

Adrien smirked. "Yeah way."

Lilith's lips curled wryly. "I can't believe I'm the only one who left the maze empty-handed."

"What do you mean?" Adrien asked.

"Arthur also got some," she said. "But I can't thank you enough. You really did this for me, huh?"

Adrien let out a low whistle. "Guess it's time you traveled to Fateland then," he said with a wink. "Let me know how it goes."

"I'm sure Jake will take detailed notes," Lilith teased.

Jake shrugged. "I know you're joking, but I already have a designated notepad just for the ritual."

"Shoo, shoo, all of you!" Professor Thomas entered the room, waving her hands like she was herding geese. "Miss Fletcher needs to rest!" Her eyes landed on Adrien. "And how did you even get in here?"

Adrien grinned. "Who can resist this face?"

Professor Thomas arched a brow. "I can." She placed a hand on her waist. "Out. Now."

Adrien sighed dramatically, backing toward the door. "Lilith, don't leave without saying goodbye, okay?"

"She's not going anywhere," Professor Thomas muttered. "What are you kids talking about?"

Lilith shook her head at Adrien's theatrics. "I won't," she promised, watching Adrien and Jake disappear into the hallway.

Once the door shut, Professor Thomas turned back, carrying a cup of warm tea. "Here, dear. Drink this. It'll help you feel better."

Lilith reached for the cup. "Thank you, Professor Thomas."

"Call me Donna," she said with a wink, eyes full of warmth.

Lilith smiled. "Thank you, Donna." She sipped, feeling its heat spread through her.

Professor Thomas pulled a chair beside the bed. "You've been through a lot," she said gently. "I want you to know—you're not alone. We're here for you." She squeezed Lilith's hand lightly. "That was a really big scare, but you're a strong young lady. Remember that."

Lilith swallowed. Professor Thomas reminded her of Meghan—someone who wouldn't sneak her candy from the top cabinet, but who'd take care of her if she got sick from too many sweets.

"I'll let you rest now, my dear," Professor Thomas added. "But don't worry—tomorrow, you'll feel like new."

Lilith nodded, and after the professor left, she found herself staring at the Hypnos Inhibitor on her wrist. *Someone must've put it there while she was unconscious. Arthur, probably, once he woke up.*

She sighed, setting the empty mug down and picking up her phone from the nightstand. It was past Amy's bedtime back home. Lilith stared at the screen, at the time zone she used to live in, at the place she used to call home. *Funny. Home didn't feel half as much like home as the Academy did.*

At *home*, she'd always been too invisible. Too odd. Too nerdy. Too young. Too shy. Too clumsy. Too serious. Too awkward.

But here—here, she was just Lilith. No more "too much" of anything. Just herself. She missed her family, but being this close to leaving the Academy hurt in a way she hadn't expected.

Her thumb hovered over an old photo of her mom. Since the memory spells had begun to crack, Nathan had started reappearing in old pictures too—half blurred in the background, as if he had been there all along and she had somehow been forced not to see him. *Would she forget him all over again when she left? Forget this place too?* She turned toward the window over her bed, heart thudding. The list for the ritual had every item checked off now. It was time—time to reach out to the Fates. Time to learn what her future held.

Could life threads be mended? Could fate be rewritten? Her grip tightened around the blanket.

What if she just... let it go? Looper life didn't have to mean death. She'd seen it: Loopers gave life as well as took it. They kept balance. *Maybe... she could do that.*

She exhaled, fingers curling into her sheets.

Or maybe not. Lilith had never been good at living with regrets. With what ifs. With the terrible itch of never knowing what might have happened if she had been brave enough to try.

She had to go through with the ritual. She had to ask the Fates if they had made a mistake.

CHAPTER TWENTY-EIGHT

THE MOIRAI'S ANSWER

B ack in her room the next night, Lilith stood on the
balcony, watching the stars flicker to life. It was almost
time. She turned back inside, her gaze lingering on Amy's
picture before exhaling softly.

A flash of gold streaked across her vision. A glowing bird
zipped through the wall, scattering into scrambled letters at her
feet. The symbols twisted, unraveled, and snapped into place.

Arthur and Jake are already there. Her pulse quickened as she scribbled a reply on her glowing wrist. A message bird of her own took flight, vanishing into the air.

On my way.

-L

Each step down the quiet hall made her heartbeat louder. *Was she really ready? Could they actually reach the Fates?*

The library was empty, shadows stretching across the shelves. Near the hidden passage, a figure moved—Arthur. He was waiting, arms crossed.

"Hey, you. Hills is already downstairs," he said, pushing open the concealed door. "Let's go."

Everything was perfectly arranged, almost an exact replica of the rituals they had studied for months. A white candle for Clotho, placed beside the spindle and the siren's feather. A red candle for Lachesis, carefully set next to the woven cloth and the minotaur's hair. A black candle for Atropos, flanked by the shears and the python's scale. All of them faced a golden-framed painting of the Fates.

Jake knelt at the edge of the ritual area, carefully finishing the golden ring with Midas Elixir.

Lilith's eyes widened. "When—and how—did you guys do all this?"

Arthur smirked, closing the entrance behind them before tossing her a white robe. "No idea what you're talking about."

Jake stood, dusting off his hands before handing her an incense stick soaked in sacred wine. His eyes gleamed with excitement. "We're ready whenever you are."

Lilith took the robe, fingers trembling as she pulled it over her clothes. This was happening. Her heart pounded—not from fear of the ritual itself, but because of everything it meant. If she went through with this... *what would she gain? Or, worse—what would she lose?*

Arthur's voice was soft, his chin lowering to meet her gaze. "You okay?"

Lilith forced a smile. "Yeah." She swallowed hard.

"You don't have to do this," he said.

"Not at all," Jake agreed quickly.

Lilith tightened her grip on the incense. "I do." Her voice was firm.

Arthur didn't press her further.

Jake took a deep breath, puffing his chest. "Well, then—let's do this." He clapped his hands once, trying to sound confident. "Everything's in place. It's gonna work—I can feel it."

Lilith nodded. Together, they pulled their hoods over their heads, casting a cleansing spell before stepping into the circle of Midas Elixir.

"Ready?" Lilith asked, standing before the candles. Arthur and Jake nodded and she snapped the incense stick into three equal parts—one for each of them. "I couldn't have done any of this without you." Her voice was barely a whisper. She swallowed hard, pushing back the lump in her throat. "Thank you."

Jake bit his lip. "In case this is the last time we see each other... just know we're gonna miss you." His voice wavered, his eyes glistening.

Lilith exhaled sharply. "Me too." And she would—if she still remembered them after this.

Steeling herself, she activated the mark on her wrist, pulling a grain of Life Powder from her pendant. The tiny spark hovered before her, shimmering in the candlelight. Arthur and Jake leaned in as she extended the incense forward, their three sticks meeting at the tips. The grain descended gracefully—landing on all three at once. A golden ember flared to life, igniting them instantly.

"Clotho, Lachesis, Atropos," their voices rang in unison.

The incense burned with a golden glow before shifting—white, red, and black—to match the candles before them.

Jake began, his voice steady. "Our fate, we place upon your weaving hands."

Arthur continued, his tone reverent. "And humbly, under the dust of life, we send you a message."

Lilith swallowed. Her heart hammered. "Let us walk the paths you have threaded, as our choices reveal the destinies ahead."

The incense sticks burned away in a flash, vanishing entirely—except for Lilith's. A tiny red spark remained in her hand, weightless yet warm. It pulsed like a flickering ember. The air thickened with the scent of mint, honey, sage, and vanilla, swirling in waves as Midas Elixir ignited around them. The golden circle pulsed, casting eerie, shifting shadows along the stone walls.

Lilith's stomach twisted. *The spell was working. Right?*

Arthur and Jake each rested a hand on her shoulders. They could tell she needed reassurance.

Lilith took a deep breath, then pulled a strand of her own hair, holding it over the tiny, pulsing ember between her fingers. She hesitated. Then—she let it fall.

The hair sizzled into the ember. Lilith closed her eyes, reciting the words they had practiced again and again.

"Moirai, I bring you my plea.

An unjust prophecy has cursed me.

Please hear my whisper.

This injustice must be seen—

To mend my destiny."

It was supposed to dissolve. But—it didn't.

Lilith opened her eyes. The ember still sat between her thumb and forefinger.

She frowned, repeating the words.

Nothing happened.

Then—she noticed it. The glow of Midas Elixir had turned blue. Her stomach tightened. That wasn't in the books.

She turned toward Arthur and Jake. *Wait—where had they gone?* Lilith's breath caught. "Guys?" Her voice wavered.

The room dimmed. Shadows bled from every corner, pooling around the golden ritual frame like ink seeping into paper. A figure stirred in the left corner, beyond the reach of the candlelight. Beyond the reach of her eyes. That shouldn't have been possible.

Her pulse spiked. A shiver crawled down her spine. "Jake?" She squinted, her Drakon-sight sharpening. The shadows twisted unnaturally at the edges, swallowing everything.

"Arthur?" Her voice cracked.

A chuckle echoed—deep, raspy, wrong. "A plea, she says," a voice rasped, rusted as if dragged across stone.

Lilith's pulse hammered. Her feet slid back on instinct.

Then, two pairs of glowing white-blue eyes blinked open. Lilith froze. If hearts could leap from chests, hers would have bolted. Behind her, the black candle flickered once, sharp and cold, but no third shadow formed. Somehow, the missing sister felt more frightening than the two who had come. Maybe because Lilith had just knocked on the door of someone who belonged to Tartarus.

Another voice slithered from the right—hoarse, like nails scraping against a chalkboard. "A very uncertain plea," it mused.

Lilith's fingers curled tight around her purifier.

Was this really the Fates? Or was this some kind of trick? No one had said anything about meeting them in person. Could it be Elizabeth somehow? Had she escaped? Was she controlling the boys again? No—impossible.

Her gaze darted between the piercing blue eyes in the shadows.

"Mend her destiny, she says, as if there could be a mistake." The first voice coiled around her, eerie and laced with amusement.

"Can you believe it, sister?" The second voice cackled. "How did she even summon us here?"

Lilith's throat went dry, staring at the eyes on her right. "L-Lachesis?" Then she glanced at the one on her left. "Clotho?"

Their stares pinned her in place. *They are here.* Lilith's pulse thundered in her ears. She was *really* standing before the Fates—actual, ancient, undeniable. She had wanted this, had prepared for it, but now, caught in their gaze, she felt like a thread dangling between their fingers, waiting to be cut.

"A human who remembers our names and recognizes which one is which." The figure on the left spoke first—Clotho, her voice a slow drag of amusement. "Perhaps you are worthy of our presence after all." A pause stretched, heavy and deliberate. "Fine. Let me hear your request, child."

It wasn't an invitation. It was a demand.

How exactly was she supposed to say: *Hi, I accidentally became a Looper, and I was wondering if I could return the gift—not because I want to leave, but because, well, the Looper thing kind of sucks. But if it's not too much trouble, I'd like to keep the other gift so I can stay at the Academy—please don't smite me?*

Before she could shape her thoughts into words, the red spark between her fingers pulsed. Then—it split in two, each fragment drifting toward opposite ends of the room, leaving a shimmering thread of life in its wake.

"Huh—Lilith Agnes Fletcher," Clotho rasped, her voice slow and deliberate. "Gifted by us from a lineage of Loopers. Protected by Persephone. Touched by Hades. Placed under Zeus's wings."

"Oh," Clotho murmured, almost to herself. "Now I see who you are." A note of understanding settled into her tone. "It all makes sense."

Lilith's breath caught. Hearing her full name from the lips of a Fate made everything feel terrifyingly real. Her knees threatened to buckle, but she locked them in place, forcing herself to stay upright.

"Sister, we should go," Lachesis cut in, her voice sharp with impatience. "Choices were made. Paths were taken. We've made no mistake. That much is clear."

"Quiet, sister." Clotho's voice cracked like a whip.

"No. You know what kind of results this can bring," Lachesis snapped, her voice rising.

"Hidden threads still exist," Clotho said. "And this one has found its way back to the loom. This was never about a mistake."

"I don't like this," Lachesis hissed. "It's Admetus all over again."

"I said it then, and I'll say it now: you must stop hiding the paths from everyone."

The weight of their argument pressed against Lilith's chest. *What were they even talking about?* Then—Clotho turned her attention back to Lilith.

"Now, as for you, child." Her gaze bore into her, making Lilith's pulse spike. "Fate is nothing but fair. So first, I'll ask you: if I placed you back in time, to the exact moment you accepted the Looper's gift—would you choose differently?"

Lilith blinked. "Can you do that?" Her voice barely rose above a whisper. "Go back in time?"

Clotho ignored the question.

"Let me help you understand, child." Life Powder flowed from her fingertips, forming a perfect image of baby Lilith. A shimmering thread unraveled from the illusion, weaving through every major event of her life. Her mother's death. The moment Nathan lay on the ground, pleading for her to accept the Fates' gift. Then—the thread split in two.

One strand followed the path Lilith had taken, leading to the Academy. The other showed her refusing the gift.

Scissors appeared.

With a single, decisive snip, both Lilith's and Nathan's life threads were severed. Lilith's breath hitched. The room seemed to shrink around her, the weight of the revelation pressing down like lead.

"Are you saying my brother and I both would have died that night if I hadn't accepted your gift?" Her voice trembled.

"It's not often that we let humans see what could have been, but you are not wrong, child." Clotho's tone remained measured, deliberate. "So I will ask you once more. If I placed you back in time, would you refuse your gift? Is that truly your heart's desire?"

Lilith swallowed hard. The word clawed its way out of her throat before she could stop it. "No."

She hadn't planned for this. She had spent months agonizing over what to say, how to plead her case. But never—not once—had she considered the possibility that this gift had saved her life.

Lachesis let out a slow, triumphant hiss. "As I said—no mistake was made."

But Clotho wasn't finished. "And yet... a choice was taken away."

Lachesis snapped toward her, bristling. "No. Don't you dare."

"You know I'm right, sister." Clotho's glowing eyes shifted for the first time since their conversation began.

Lachesis growled. "Don't put words in my mouth." A beat. "But do it if you must."

Clotho's gaze locked onto Lilith. "Because an innocent was made to carry a punishment that was never hers, we are willing to set one wrong right."

Lilith's throat tightened. "What do you mean?"

Clotho hummed, almost amused. "Oh, child, I'm offering to mend a wrong—one that does not belong to you." Her voice was slow, deliberate. "Which is quite noble. A true desire that harms no soul already gone."

She paused. "Think deeply, and I shall grant your wish."

Lilith's mind raced. There were so many things she wanted, so many wrongs she wished she could undo. But in the pit of her stomach, she already knew. "Arthur." The name left her lips before she could second-guess it.

Clotho inclined her head. "The boy, indeed."

Lilith's breath caught. "You can bring Arthur's sister back? Change his past?"

A sharp, high-pitched laugh pierced the air. Lachesis. The sheer delight in her screech made Lilith's bones rattle. "Oh, child," Clotho said, unfazed, "that soul is long gone—powder, flesh, and thread. Not even Hades would call her back from the path she has taken."

Lilith's stomach twisted. "Then... what wrong are you talking about?"

Clotho's glowing eyes flickered. "You were close. The wrong is not yours. But your thread is tangled with it. You may walk away with your answer, or you may spend this moment mending a burden another soul should never have carried."

Lilith's breath hitched. "Arthur's mother." *It had to be.* Her pulse slammed against her ribs. *If Nicole was innocent, then who was guilty?*

Lachesis hissed softly. Clotho's glowing eyes did not blink.

"If she's innocent," she whispered, "then why is she still there?"

"Because truth is not the same as justice," Clotho said. "And justice is not always brave enough to find the truth."

"So, you would release his mother and punish whoever was guilty?"

"We are releasing the innocent," Clotho corrected, her voice unwavering. "Not acting as jury or executioner for the guilty."

Lilith's mind spun. *Arthur's mother could be... free?* She exhaled slowly. At the very least, bringing Nicole home had to be better than leaving Arthur with nothing but that man who called himself a father.

Clotho's voice was patient but firm. "Child, you are exactly where you were meant to be. You know the right answer. Give it to us."

Lilith swallowed. "Okay. We have a deal." She released the breath she hadn't realized she was holding. "Bring Arthur's mom back."

A flicker of something—*approval?*—passed through Clotho's glowing eyes. "I knew this was the choice your thread would reach for, child."

With a fluid motion, Clotho raised a hand, burning the shimmering thread that had connected Lilith to the sisters.

The ember-like glow spiraled upward before vanishing.

"Our deal is done and sealed. A choice has been made. Your destiny does not need mending. When your friend returns home, his mother shall be there to greet him."

A sharp huff echoed through the chamber. "I shall never understand humans."

"I said quiet, sister!" Clotho barked.

"Farewell, Lilith Agnes Fletcher."

The shadows stirred. And just like that—they were gone.

CHAPTER TWENTY-NINE

BEYOND THE THREADS

L ilith blinked. The room was silent, still. The painting of the
Fates stared back at her. Lilith's fingers curled around the
burnt-out incense in her hand. Somehow, the hood of her white
robe had slipped back onto her shoulders. She rubbed her fingers
together, missing the cozy warmth of the spark that had been
between them. The sweet, minty scent of the ritual still lingered
in the air.

"What now?" Jake's voice cut through the haze, grounding
her. "The offerings are gone, so I'd assume it worked, right?" he

asked, scratching his forehead and glancing around. "The message was... delivered?"

Lilith shook her head slowly, as if waking from a dream. The room felt different—tilted, like the world hadn't fully settled back into place.

"Of course it was. Now we sit tight and see if it worked," Arthur said with a shrug.

"Preferably while eating pancakes, right?" Jake grinned, trying to lighten the mood.

Lilith swallowed. "A-actually, they came here."

Arthur's gaze sharpened. "What do you mean?"

"The Fates. I mean, not all of them. Only Clotho and Lachesis. We talked." Saying the words aloud made them harder to believe.

Jake inhaled sharply, then sniffed the air. "Did we, uh... accidentally inhale oracle fumes in here or something?" Jake's eyes widened after a second. "Wait! Are you serious? You actually talked to the Fates? Like, face-to-face?"

Lilith exhaled, shaking her head. "The circle of Midas Elixir turned blue, you guys disappeared, and then—*poof*. The Fates showed up."

"Whoa," Jake mouthed, clearly stunned. "That's crazy! What did they say? What did you say? What did they look like? Where did we go? How come we didn't notice? Do you still have your gift?" He grabbed Lilith's arm, flipping it over to check her wrist.

"Hold your herbs, Hills." Arthur lifted his hand in a calming gesture before shifting his gaze to Lilith. "Are you okay, Fletcher?"

Lilith nodded and took a slow, steady breath. *What was she supposed to say?* She couldn't tell Arthur she had made a deal with the Fates to bring his mother home—she didn't want him to owe her anything. *But what if Jake sensed she was hiding something?* She chewed her bottom lip, organizing her thoughts. "Well, they asked if I would've denied my gift the night of the accident," she began.

"And you said yes, right?" Jake looked like a kid listening to a thrilling bedtime story, while Arthur stayed silent.

Lilith hesitated. "I thought about it. But then they showed me what would've happened if I hadn't accepted my gift." A shiver ran down her spine at the memory. "And it involved some unexpected snipping of life threads—including mine."

Jake's excitement deflated. "Oh."

Lilith forced a shrug. "So, since I wouldn't have changed my answer... I guess I was always supposed to be a Looper." She lifted her brows slightly, hoping to brush it off.

Jake stared for a beat, searching for more, but then his focus shifted. "What did *they* look like?"

Lilith pursed her lips. "I only saw their eyes. Creepy and glowing eyes."

Jake groaned. "Seriously? Only eyes?"

"Pretty much." She shrugged, watching the flicker of disappointment cross his face.

Then—Jake's face lit up again. "Wait! That means—Lilith is staying!" He threw his hands up.

Lilith high-fived him playfully. "That's right."

Clotho and Lachesis were right about one thing: Lilith was exactly where she was supposed to be. Her fate hadn't changed, but for the first time, it didn't feel like a curse.

She had stood before the Fates, spoken her truth, and walked away with something good—Arthur's mother was coming home.

Over the following days, Lilith tried to spend as much time as possible with her friends. One evening, just before they were set to leave for the school break, the three of them lounged near the Phaunos Tree—the very place where their adventure had begun.

Jake suddenly shot upright, eyes wide. "WAIT—Lilith! I finally figured out where your second gift came from!"

Lilith raised an eyebrow. "What are you talking about?"

Jake grinned. "Do you remember what Clotho said?" He pulled a small, well-worn notebook from his pocket—the one where he scribbled down every detail Lilith had managed to share with them.

Arthur rolled his eyes. "Protected by *Persephone*," he said, as if the answer had been obvious.

Her breath caught. "Yeah. But—" Lilith's voice trailed off as the pieces clicked into place all at once.

Her gifts. The Drakon-sight. The way she could manipulate plants. And she probably should have picked up on the whole geokinesis thing when she *accidentally* split the ground open under Christopher Fox after he picked on her during Teams 101 finals.

Lilith inhaled sharply. "No way."

Jake grinned. "Yes way."

Arthur smirked. "Took you two long enough to figure that out."

"You knew and didn't tell me?" Lilith shook her head. *Persephone. Nature and the underworld. Life and death. Somehow, it fit.*

Arthur brushed dirt from his pants. "Why would I spoil the fun?" He raised an eyebrow. "Anyway, we should get going."

As they walked, Lilith absently ran her fingers over the Hypnos Inhibitor around her wrist. They had finally found out Rose was the one who had left it by Lilith's door, a quiet token of gratitude for saving her baby. But even Jake couldn't explain how Rose had found a relic rare enough to make his voice squeak.

The Academy buzzed with students saying their goodbyes. Together, they made their way to the transition room—the final stop before returning to the real world.

Jake's mom waved from one of the many portals. "Jay-Jay! Over here, sweetie!"

Jake beamed. "Coming, Mom!" He turned to them. "Gotta go!" He wrapped Lilith in a tight hug and waved to Arthur.

"I'm gonna miss you!" she called as his portal closed behind him.

Arthur adjusted his bag. "Well, my father doesn't like waiting." Then, for a brief second, he hesitated. And with the faintest smirk, he said, "Having two first-year teammates wasn't so bad. See you soon, Fletcher."

Lilith held his gaze. "It won't be soon enough."

Arthur stepped through the portal and froze. A woman stood on the other side, one hand pressed to her mouth, staring at Arthur like she'd been waiting years to see him. Then the portal vanished.

"LILYYYYYYYYYYYYY!" Amy's voice rang through the entire transition room.

Lilith turned just in time to see her little sister bouncing on her toes beside Dad and Meghan, waving wildly from the airport arrival gate on the other side of the portal. Her heart swelled. She ducked under the handrail just in time to catch Amy as she launched herself forward.

"I MISSED YOU SO MUCH!" Amy shouted at the top of her lungs.

Lilith laughed, catching her midair. "I missed you too, Cricket."

Amy giggled, clinging to her. "You have to tell me everything."

Lilith smirked. "You wouldn't believe it even if I told you."

Amy grinned. "But you're gonna tell me anyway, right?"

Lilith ruffled her hair before pulling her in for another hug. And, as the sun dipped below the horizon, she smiled.

For the first time, leaving didn't feel like losing something. It felt like knowing exactly where she belonged.

Thank you for reading Lilith Fletcher and the Threads of Fate. If you'd like to share your thoughts, please consider leaving an honest review wherever you purchased this book. Help other readers decide whether this magical adventure is right for them! Your support means everything! Let's stay in touch: @writerversejourney

U.S. Direct Review:

amazon.com/review/create-review?asin=B0DWXZ RVXX

MANGA SNEAK PEEK

Have you ever read a manga? If not, now's your chance! I'm thinking about creating a Lilith Fletcher manga, and I'd love to hear what you think! Oh, and a quick tip—manga is read from right to left, so be sure to follow along the right way!

Ready? Check the next few pages >>>

And remember: mangas are read from RIGHT to LEFT!

I can't wait to meet you again! Brace yourselves for Lilith
Fletcher: Book 2!

Want to dive deeper into mythology & magic?
Explore more books & resources at: bit.ly/writerverse

Bonus Content - Characters

Adrien

Jake

Artie

LILITH FLETCHER

NATHAN

AMY

MEGHAN

NICHOLAS

F un Fact: Lilith's First Adventure

Did you know that Lilith Fletcher has been in the making for over a decade? Before becoming this book, Lilith's story began as a serialized adventure, with readers following episodes as they released. That means Lilith has already traveled through more than one kind of storytelling magic—and this book is only the beginning.

Here's a sneak peek at the impact Lilith's story made while the platform was still running:

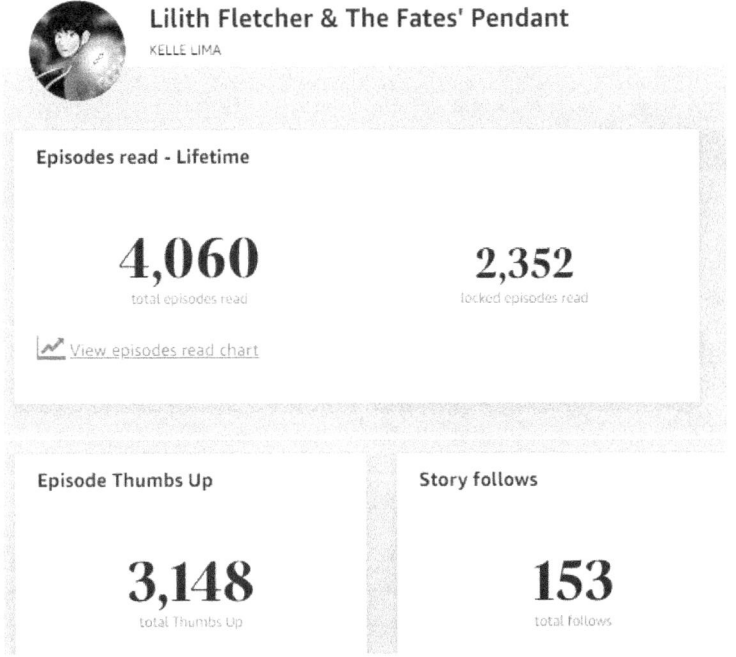

Lilith Fletcher & The Fates' Pendant
KELLE LIMA

Episodes read - Lifetime

4,060
total episodes read

2,352
locked episodes read

View episodes read chart

Episode Thumbs Up

3,148
total Thumbs Up

Story follows

153
total follows

ABOUT THE AUTHOR!

Kelle Lima is an author, illustrator, educator, and storyteller who brings mythology, adventure, and magic to life in books for young readers. Passionate about blending history, folklore, and fast-paced storytelling, she crafts action-packed tales that keep young readers on the edge of their seats.

A lifelong lover of ancient myths and epic quests, Kelle is originally from Brazil and draws inspiration from Greek mythology, weaving timeless legends into modern, relatable adventures for today's readers. Kelle is also an educator and game designer, and uses her background to create books that challenge young minds, spark curiosity, and encourage exploration. As a single mom and entrepreneur, she built her publishing journey from the ground up, driven by her passion for helping kids discover the power of stories.

Beyond mythic tales, she also loves spending time with her daughter, playing board games, doing crafts, and binging her favorite series and movies.

Want more mythology, magic, and behind-the-scenes extras?
Visit: bit.ly/writerverse
Follow: @writerversejourney